VOID

/32716

U.S. ARMY
SPECIAL FORCES

FRED J. PUSHIES

MBI Publishing
Company

Dedicated to
The Warriors:
The Soldiers of the U.S. Army Special Forces

First published in 2001 by MBI Publishing Company, Galtier Plaza, Suite 200, 380 Jackson Street, St. Paul, MN 55101-3885 USA

MBI Publishing Company books are also available at discounts in bulk quantity for industrial or sales-promotional use. For details write to Special Sales Manager at Motorbooks International Wholesalers & Distributors, Galtier Plaza, Suite 200, 380 Jackson Street, St. Paul, MN 55101-3885 USA.

Library of Congress Cataloging-in-Publication Data

    Pushies, Fred J.
       U.S. Army Special Forces / Fred J. Pushies
         p. cm. — (The power series)
       Includes index.
        ISBN 0-7603-0862-4 (pbk. alk. paper)
          1. United States. Army. Special Forces—History.
          2. United States. Army—Commando troops. I. Title.
         II. Power series (Osceola, Wis.)
    UA34.S64 P87 2001
    356'.167'0973—dc21   2001030594

On the front cover:
If you are the enemy, the last thing you want is a heavily armed Green Beret lurking in the woods around your compound. Where there is one, there are usually more nearby. Here a team member carefully aims his weapon, ready to fire single rifle rounds, automatic bursts, or grenades.

On the frontispiece:
Phase III—Robin Sage is where all the training comes together. The SF students are matched up into functional A-Teams, or ODAs, and sent into Pineland. Here they will put to use the skills set they have learned, and discover whether they have what it takes to wear the green beret.

On the title page:
Each soldier is a mature, physically rugged, morally straight, thoroughly lethal, and highly skilled individual who brings a new level of professionalism to an already elite military unit.

On the back cover:
Special Forces Advance Reconnaissance, Target Analysis, and Exploitation Techniques Course (SFARTAETC) provides the basic entry-level training in precision marksmanship, integrated CQB, and interpretability with other specifically designated forces. Here, a squad "knocks" on a door before entering.

All photographs are the author's, Fred J. Pushies unless otherwise noted.

Edited by Michael Haenggi

Printed in China

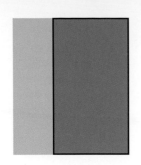

Contents

Foreword

This book pays tribute to a special breed of man, a special breed of Americans, and a special breed of warrior. Special Forces soldiers, commonly referred to as the "Green Berets," are unique—not only due to the types of missions they undertake, the rigorous training they undergo, or the equipment they use, but also because of their character, spirit, and dedication. They are men who step away from conventional methods and conventional thinking to undertake tasks that many experts would deem impossible. They are men who can be ruthless in their quest to accomplish a mission, yet selfless and compassionate, caring for people who are in desperate need of a helping hand. I know this from firsthand experience. I will always be grateful to have had the opportunity to serve alongside, and to be associated with, such courageous and awe-inspiring men.

Although officially only 49 years old, the Green Berets can trace their proud lineage back to the daring and courage of Americans serving in the Revolutionary War. Since the Special Forces inception in 1952, the Green Berets have been at the forefront of nearly every operation involving America's military, from Korea to Vietnam, from Grenada and Panama to Iraq, and from Somalia and Haiti to the Balkans. Often the Green Berets are the United States' only military presence in a number of countries around the world. They stand as both America's vanguard and its goodwill ambassadors. The renaissance men of warfare, Special Forces stand ready to undertake any mission, from unconventional warfare, direct action, and rescue missions to peace operations and humanitarian assistance. Our Special Forces provide unique capabilities that are essential to the United States' national security strategy and its ability to provide leadership in an uncertain and troubled world.

Since the creation of the Special Operations Command in 1987, a unified command with headquarters at MacDill Air Force Base in Tampa, Florida, Special Forces has become a vital element of joint and combined military operations. Each regional Commander in Chief (CinC), which includes European Command, Pacific Command, Southern Command, Central Command, and Joint Forces Command, has a Special Operations component manned with Special Forces soldiers. The Green Berets provide forces to conduct operations across the spectrum of conflict as well as the staff expertise to better integrate their unique capabilities and talents into joint and combined operations around the world.

The trend to greater integration is important. The men of the Green Berets and their colleagues in the Special Operations community are recognized not only for their ability to conduct missions for which they are uniquely qualified, but also as a great combat multiplier during conventional military operations.

The future of Special Forces will be tied to its ability to continue to attract and develop quality personnel, as well as maintain its standards of excellence. The United States relies on its technological prowess to stay ahead of potential adversaries—and Special Forces will leverage that technology. But it is the spirit, ingenuity, and professionalism of each individual who wears the Green Beret that maintains the force's vital core, ensuring its long-term efficacy. They are extraordinary men whom we ask to accomplish what others would often consider impossible. As this book underscores, it is the extraordinary caliber of the individual Green Berets that has been the constant source of strength for this incomparable organization. The men who constitute its ranks will continue to be the underlying and undying strength of the Special Forces as it meets the challenges of the new millennium.

De Oppresso Liber!

—*General Henry H. Shelton*
Chairman of the Joint Chiefs of Staff

Acknowledgments

First and foremost, I must acknowledge my thanks to God for His guidance and wisdom in this project. To Michael Haenggi, editor at Motorbooks International; General Henry H. Shelton, Chairman of the Joint Chiefs of Staff; Lt. Colonel Thomas Rheinlander, Carol Darby, Barbara Ashley, SFC Amanda Glenn, Specialist John Creese, U.S. Army Special Operations Command -Public Affairs Office, Ft. Bragg; Major Tom McCollum, Captain Andrew "Dutch" Franz, Major Jonathan B. Withington, Special Forces - PAO, Ft. Bragg; Major Rich Patterson, Special Warfare Center - PAO, Ft. Bragg; Randy Action, President & CEO, U.S. Cavalry; Lt. Colonel Mike Nagata, Major Jack Jensen, Major Patrick Eberhart, Major Douglas Robertson, Command Sergeant Major Melvin Lyles, Staff Sergeant Peter Simchuk, Training Cadre - 1st Special Warfare Training Group; Command Sergeant Major Richard Fitzgerald - Non-Commissioned Officers Academy; Lt. Colonel Clifford C. Cloonan, MC, U.S. Army; Commander Michael Wilkinson, MSC, U.S. Navy; Captain Steve Ellison, MC, U.S. Army Joint Special Operations Medical Training Center; Major Kimm Rowe - Range 37; Mr. Donald Strassburg, Special Forces Arms Facility; Major Thomas Hartzel; CWO4 "Bulldog" Balwanz; Roxanne Merritt - JFKSWC Museum Curator; Mr. Joe Lupyak, CSM (ret.); Mr. David Clarke, CSM (ret.); Cadre 1st SWTG, Colonels "Daniels, Ranger & Mosby" G-Chiefs of Pineland; ODA 914 & ODA 916; Mrs. Catherine Bank; Mr. Noel Corby - Operations - National Training Center, Ft. Irwin; Gordon Sims, President, 1st Special Service Force Association; Colonel Mike Jones - Commander; Major Jeff Kent; Major Craig Johnson; C Company 3rd Battalion: Colonel Jack Zeigler; Major Ken Cobb; Captain Brent Jorgenson; Captain Mike Irvine; ODA-391, ODA-392, & ODA-395, MSgt. Gary Kenitzer, 3rd Special Forces Group (Airborne); CWO2 Michael Roth; MSG Sam Wright; SSG J. DeVerteuil; ODA-774, 7th Special Forces Group (Airborne) A Company 3rd Battalion; ODA-581, Colonel Gary Danley Commander 3rd Battalion, 5th Special Forces Group (Airborne); ODA-052, ODA-055, & ODA-065, Lt. Colonel David Alegre 10th Special Forces Group (Airborne) Company C, 2nd Battalion; Lt. Colonel Daniel Moore G7 Force Integration - USASFC(A); Major Richard Steiner, S-3, 2nd Battalion, 3rd Special Forces Group (Airborne); Captain Drew Bayliss, CWO2 Ken Hodges, SFC David A. Harrington, and ODA-363; SOTIC instructors, NCOIC - MSG Bill Olson, SFC Ron Woolett, SFC George Simmons, SFC Jim Wallace, SFC Dave Garner, Rick Boucher, MSgt. (ret.), Cpl. George Bundy, 2nd Rangers and SSgt. Clifford Richardson, 5th Special Forces Group (Airborne) ODA-546; Captain Brent Epperson - Assistant S-3, Sgt. Mark Williams, Multimedia, NCOIC, 7th Special Forces Group (Airborne); Mr. Emit B. Hutsman, Curator, Ft. Clark Museum - Indian Scouts; Colonel Robert S. Sumner USA (ret.) Alamo Scouts, 6th Army; Robert E. Passanisi, Historian, Merrill's Marauder Association; Mr. Richard Sanne; Mary Scott Smith, Vice President, Barret Firearms Manufacturing, Inc.; Michael J. Winey, Curator, U.S. Army Military History Institute; John W. Goldtrap, Rebe Phillips, General Atomics Aeronautical Systems, Inc.; Kathy Vinson, Defense Visual Information Center; Steve Harrigan, Johnson Controls World Service, Inc. Also Darren Proctor, Robert Bentley Jr., and my family.

Special Thanks to "The Sea Pigs": Captain Brian Ebert, CW2 Tony Bonnell, MSG B.F. Burnham, SFC Mikel Chapman, SSG Jason Clark, SSG Jeremy Jemmett, Sgt. Joe Ferris, SSG Jason Perkins, SSG Doug Peterson, and SFC Greg Green of ODA-173, 1st Special Forces Group (Airborne).

Introduction

Unconventional warfare is nothing new. The Old Testament recounts the story of Gideon, whom God told to do battle with the Midianites approximately 5,500 years ago. The Midianites, an enemy of Israel, had a force so large their numbers were uncountable. Gideon began his campaign with 32,000 men, but twice God told him to reduce the ranks of his troops. Finally, when Gideon's force numbered only 300, God gave him a plan and set the attack in motion.

Gideon divided the 300 men into three companies of 100 each. He armed them each with a trumpet, an empty pitcher and a lamp, which was placed inside the pitcher. During the night the three companies secretly took up preordained positions, surrounding the enemy. Just around midnight, when the Midianites had placed the first watch, Gideon and his men blew their trumpets, broke the pitchers, and raised their lamps. In the ensuing confusion that befell the enemy, the Midianites turned their swords on one another, as Gideon and his band disappeared into the night. This encounter foreshadowed future unconventional methods: employ psychological warfare, stealth, and lightening hit-and-run tactics.

Some 5,000 years later, in 218 BC, a young commander named Hannibal employed yet another facet of unconventional warfare. Hannibal marched his men, roughly 35,000 troops, over the Italian Alps. While such a movement is not unusual, what was unexpected and well out of the ordinary was the fact that Hannibal's invasion force included elephants. To move huge equatorial animals through the frozen expanses of the mountains would be unthinkable today—and it was unthinkable then. Hannibal added more principles for unconventional warfare: Do the unexpected, tackle the impossible, and succeed at all costs.

Unconventional warfare has been with mankind since the beginning of time. In Greek mythology the Greek warriors feigned retreat and sailed away, leaving behind a large wooden horse. The Trojans believed it was an offering to the goddess Athena, and brought it into the city for luck. Unbeknownst to the jubilant Trojans, the Greeks were hidden inside. As the city slept, the Greeks slipped from the horse, now within the enemy's fortress, opened the city's gates to the returning sailors, and decimated the Trojan forces.

The legendary Trojan Horse was featured on the beret crest when the U.S. Army Special Forces troops carried out postwar activities in 1952 Germany. It was used again in the formation of U.S. Special Operations Command in the 1980s. Currently, the representation of the Trojan Horse embodied in the knight piece can be found on the beret crest of the U.S. Army Special Warfare Center/School. A symbol of unconventional warfare from ancient times, it continues in the heraldry of the modern Special Forces warrior.

From its humble beginnings as a handful of men roaming the Bavarian Alps of post–World War II Germany, the Special Forces has evolved into a critical component of U.S. military operations. Whether performing civic actions and training with the indigenous populace or carrying out clandestine activities in denied territory, these men epitomize the term *warriors*, and bring unconventional warfare to a new level. This is their story—where they have come from, and where they are heading in the new millennium. These are the men of the U.S. Army Special Forces, "The Quiet Professionals."

Special Forces Lineage

The lineage of today's Special Forces soldier begins some two centuries ago in an emerging country called America. It was here during the French and Indian War (1754–1763) that colonists would serve with British forces. In 1756, Major Robert Rogers recruited these Americans into a unit that would number nine companies of men. Although Maj. Rogers did not invent the unconventional warfare techniques, he did

The forerunner of the current Special Forces, Francis Marion, was known as the "Swamp Fox." He and his men brought unconventional warfare tactics to the Revolutionary War, making guerrilla raids against the British. *South Caroliniana Library*

exploit the tactics and establish them into Ranger doctrine. He is credited by some with writing the first Ranger Manual.

The newly founded Ranger companies would learn to assimilate these techniques. Following Rogers' command, they would strike where the enemy least expected them to hit, and they would traverse terrain conventional forces would avoid. The Rangers employed stealth and secrecy in their movements on the enemy. Once in position they would spring the attack and, like a North American rattlesnake, hit fast and hit hard. Major Rogers instituted a plan of action to train his Rangers and personally watched over its execution. He set strict orders for his troops to follow, stressing operational security, readiness, and tactics.

Rogers' tactics contained more than two dozen paragraphs detailing the Rangers' operational techniques. Over the years these techniques have been summarized in what has come to be known as the "Standing Orders—Rogers' Rangers." They are:

1. Don't forget nothing.

2. Have your musket clean as a whistle, hatchet scoured, sixty rounds powder and ball, and be ready to march at a minute's warning.

3. When you're on the march, act the way you would if you was sneaking up on a deer. See the enemy first.

4. Tell the truth about what you see and what you do. There is an army depending on us for correct information. You can lie all you please

when you tell other folks about the Rangers, but don't never lie to a Ranger of office.

5. Don't never take a chance you don't have to.

6. When we're on the march we march single file, far enough apart so one shot can't go through two men.

7. If we strike swamps, or soft ground, we spread out abreast, so it's hard to track us.

8. When we march, we keep moving till dark, so as to give the enemy the least possible chance at us.

9. When we camp, half the party stays awake while the other half sleeps.

10. If we take prisoners, we keep 'em separate till we have had time to examine them, so they can't cook up a story between 'em.

11. Don't ever march home the same way. Take a different route so you won't be ambushed.

12. No matter whether we travel in big parties or little ones, each party has to keep a scout 20 yards ahead, 20 yards on each flank, and 20 yards in the rear so the main body can't be surprised and wiped out.

13. Every night you'll be told where to meet if surrounded by a superior force.

14. Don't sit down to eat without posting sentries.

15. Don't sleep beyond dawn. Dawn's when the French and Indians attack.

16. Don't cross a river by a regular ford.

17. If somebody's trailing you, make a circle, come back onto your own track, and ambush the folks that aim to ambush you.

18. Don't stand up when the enemy's coming against you. Kneel down, lie down, hide behind a tree.

19. Let the enemy come till he's almost close enough to touch, then let him have it and jump out and finish him up with your hatchet.

Rogers' Rangers and these rules lay the groundwork for future generations of Special Operations Forces of the United States.

The tradition of the Rangers continued when the time came for the colonists to fight for their independence during the American Revolution. Active during the Revolutionary War were Dan Morgan's "Corps of Rangers," formed under orders from George Washington, and the Connecticut Rangers, under the leadership of Thomas Knowlton. While Morgan's men were considered expert marksmen, Knowlton's Rangers, a force of hand-picked men, were skilled in reconnaissance techniques.

It was Francis Marion, however, who would bring guerrilla war to the British and establish a firm position in the Special Forces lineage. Born and raised in South Carolina, Francis Marion fought the Cherokee Indians in 1760 as a lieutenant in the militia. During the Cherokee War, Marion learned the fighting techniques of the Indians, how they would initiate a surprise attack and then fade away as quickly as they had begun the assault. After the war Marion retired from service to take up the quiet, peaceful life of a farmer.

The war for independence changed these plans. Due to his past experience fighting the Cherokee, Marion received a commission as captain in the Continental Army and took up arms in the fight for freedom. Eventually, Marion would be promoted to the rank of General.

When Charleston fell to the British, Marion escaped capture and, like the Cherokee Indians he had fought, headed into the South Carolina swamps. Once in the swamp he established his base camp and with 150 men formed what would become known as Marion's Brigade. As the war progressed Marion and his men carried out

The U.S. Scouts, or Indian Scouts, were the first to employ the crossed arrows for their unit insignia in August 1890. Later, in World War II, the 1st Special Service Force would adopt the insignia. The crossed arrows continued their appearance in the SF beret crest and became the ensign of the U.S. Army Special Forces when the Army designated them as a separate branch in 1987. *Ft. Clark Museum*

unconventional warfare tactics against the British. They would ambush British troops, attack their supply lines, and perform hit-and-run raids on the enemy's camps; when done they would fade away into the dark forbidding recesses of the swamps. Try as they might, the British found it futile to attempt to follow these guerrillas into their safe haven of the swamp. A British colonel dubbed Marion the Swamp Fox.

Guerilla and unconventional war tactics reappeared in the U.S. Civil War. Mean's Rangers of the Union Army and Ashby's Rangers of the Confederacy were specialists in scouting, harassing, and raiding. Each did its best to hamper the efforts of the other side. Yet the best-known unconventional warfare troops of this war undeniably were the Confederate Army's Mosby's Rangers. Under the command of Colonel John Singleton Mosby of Virginia, Mosby's Rangers operated behind Union lines, just south of the Potomac. Col. Mosby began with a three-man scout element in

1862. By 1865, Mosby's Rangers had evolved into a force of eight companies of guerrillas.

Col. Mosby was a firm believer in the use of reconnaissance, aggressive action, and surprise attacks. Mosby and his Rangers cut off Union communications and supply lines, wrecked railroads, and raided base camps behind enemy lines. One of their greatest feats was to capture Union General Edwin H. Stoughton by bluffing their way into, and removing him from, his own house. Due to his stealth and uncanny ability to avoid capture, Mosby earned the nickname the Gray Ghost. Mosby's Rangers were well trained and well disciplined, setting a standard for future unconventional warfare forces.

In the years following the Civil War, American "Horse Soldiers" fought in the Great Plains Wars of the Southwest. Aware that hostile forces could not be tracked down by the cavalry alone, the U.S. Army created a new special operations force, known as the Indian Scouts. Drawn primarily from Pawnee, Navajo, and Seminole tribes, they were deployed at length all through the West. The Indian Scouts aided General G. Crook in capturing Geronimo.

With attributes comparable to today's Special Forces soldiers, these Indians Scouts were renowned in such military traits as tracking, field craft, physical courage, and boldness. The language skills, cultural appreciation, and civic action that characterized these forces are quite similar to today's Army Special Forces. The heritage of the Indian Scouts continued in the Crossed Arrows insignia that was adopted by the 1st Special Service Force during World War II.

The history of the U.S. Army Special Forces may be traced to the pre–Revolutionary War time period; however, a more direct lineage and organizational relationship follows from the elite U.S. military forces operating during World War II. Special operations units were active in all theaters of operations, from the jungles of Pacific islands,

Burma, and China, to the expanses of European mountains, woodlands, and towns.

The Second World War added the term Army Rangers to the annals of military history, and to the pages of Special Forces heraldry. Major General Lucian K. Truscott, the U.S. Army liaison to the British General Staff, submitted the idea of an American unit similar to the British Commandos to General George Marshall. The War Department responded with cables to Truscott and Major General Russell P. Hartle, commander of all Army forces in Northern Ireland, authorizing formation of the special unit.

General Truscott liked the term "commandos," but it was a British name and he desired something more American. Looking back on the history of unconventional warfare, Truscott found American troops that met the highest standards of courage, motivation, tenacity, fighting spirit, and ruggedness. The group that inspired him was that commanded by Major Rogers, and a new name was added to the U.S. military—Army Rangers.

General Hartle picked Captain William O. Darby, who had been serving as his aide-de-camp, to recruit, select, and organize the newly formed unit. Darby, a West Point graduate, was intelligent and enthusiastic, demonstrating the capacity to gain the confidence of his superiors and the loyalty of his men. Promoted to Major, Darby took on the task in hand. Major Darby and his handpicked staff officers interviewed volunteers from the 1st Armored Division, the 34th Infantry Division, and other units from the area.

Within a few weeks, the first unit of Army Rangers was selected. On 19 June 1942, in Carrickfergus, Ireland, the 1st U.S. Army Ranger Battalion was activated under the command of Major William O. Darby. This unit would come to be known as Darby's Rangers.

Major Darby and his Rangers would spend three months at the Commando Training Center at Achnacarry, Scotland. Here, under the tutelage of combat-seasoned British Commandos, the American Rangers learned the basics of unconventional warfare. Out of 600 men that began the training with Darby, 500 remained.

Darby's Rangers fought throughout Western Europe, but they achieved their greatest recognition on D-Day, 6 June 1944. The Rangers would scale the cliffs of Pointe du Hoc as part of the Allied invasion of Normandy.

The 1st Special Service Force was officially established at Fort William Henry Harrison, Montana, on 9 July 1942. These unconventional warfare troops comprised both American and Canadian soldiers under the command of Colonel Robert T. Frederick. The 1st SSF was a

Portrait of Brigadier General Robert T. Frederick, commander of the 1st Special Service Force. Known as the "Devil's Brigade," these unconventional warfare troops were constituted of both American and Canadian soldiers. *JFK Special Warfare Museum*

March 1944, at Laganga/Walawbum area, Burma. One of the 5307th's Battalion's I & R (Intelligence & Reconnaissance) Platoons, patrolling the area before the attack at Walawbum. (The 3rd Battalion consisted of two Combat Teams, Orange and Khaki, each with its own I & R Platoon.) Note the men are not carrying their field packs, so they can move about and conceal themselves more easily. *Lt. David Lubin Merrill's Marauders Association*

force of three battalion-size units, with 60 percent of the men coming from the ranks of the American military. Volunteers were sought out from various units; in some cases commanders eagerly "volunteered" some of their troublesome soldiers and sent them out to Montana. Col. Frederick weeded out men who arrived less than highly motivated, from which one could argue he was responsible for instituting the first Special Forces Assessment and Selection (SFAS). As Gordon Sims, president of the 1st Special Service Force Association, relates, "Many people think the American soldiers were roughnecks and yard birds. The truth was, some of these men were more at home in the field than in garrison. What regular Army commanders saw as troublesome actually turned out to be some of the best operators."

Col. Frederick formulated a training schedule for his men that would stress physical conditioning, hand-to-hand combat, weapons training, demolitions, infantry tactics, and mountain work. The soldiers of the 1st SSF were also airborne trained, and schooled in skiing and winter operations. Their specialty was close-quarter combat against numerically superior forces.

The 1st Special Service Force would see combat against the Japanese in the Aleutians and with the Germans in Italy and France. It was in Europe that the 1st SSF got its nickname, the Devil's Brigade. The crossed arrows and distinctive unit insignia of the present-day Special Forces was first authorized to be worn by the 1st SSF by the Secretary of War.

While Darby's Rangers and the Devil's Brigade were conducting their operations in Europe, another group of men was writing its lessons into the journal of unconventional warfare in the Pacific. Here the men of the 5307th Composite Unit (Provisional), under the leadership of Brigadier General Frank Merrill, brought the war to the Japanese in the jungles of Burma.

Organized in 1943, this unit of 3,000 men, all volunteers, was tasked with the mission of long-range infiltration behind Japanese lines. Their objective was to destroy the enemies "jugular"—their communications and supply lines. Furthermore, they were to harass and attack the Japanese at will. This unit would come to be known as Merrill's Marauders.

One of the Marauders' greatest undertakings was the seizure of the Myitkyina Airfield. Merrill and his men infiltrated through the hot, humid, insect- and disease-ridden Burmese jungle. And that was the good news. These unconventional warriors were constantly outnumbered by the enemy, and support was almost nonexistent. Merrill's Marauders' accomplishments are legendary and inspirational, even by today's standards.

Another unconventional raiding force operating in the Pacific was the Alamo Scouts. This unit of highly skilled soldiers was created by Lt. General Walter Krueger, commanding General of the U.S. Sixth Army. Those who volunteered for assignment to this force went through six weeks of arduous training and field exercises encompassing land navigation, hand-to-hand combat, weapons, communications, survival, small boat operations, and advance patrolling techniques. Those who graduated from the training were selected to become Alamo Scouts and formed into small teams, usually one officer and six or seven enlisted men.

These teams would infiltrate the numerous Japanese-held islands throughout the South Pacific, emerging from PT boats and rubber rafts to perform their missions. Their primary mission was originally reconnaissance, but their skills and the demands of war led them to greater challenges. In one of their foremost missions, the Scouts led U.S. Rangers and Filipino guerrillas in an attack on a Japanese prison camp at Cabantuan, freeing all 511 Allied prisoners there. Never numbering more than 70 men, the Alamo Scouts

Team leaders of the Alamo Scouts, left to right: Lt. Bill Nellist, Lt. Tom Roonsaville, Lt. Robert "Red" Sumner, Lt. Jack Dove. Leyte, Philippine Islands, January 1945. In more than 100 missions, the Alamo Scouts never lost a man. *Alamo Scout Association*

conducted more than a hundred missions without the loss of a single soldier.

These unconventional units of World War II were indeed U.S. Army elites. They took the principles founded by Rogers' Rangers and gave them a twentieth-century application, thus establishing a basis for modern special operations forces. Their mission was simple: Hit the enemy, hit them hard with lightning attacks, and disappear into the countryside, whether the mountains and woodlands of Europe, or the jungles of Burma. In addition to units employing lightning raids on the enemy, World War II produced another kind of unconventional warrior—a soldier who could adapt and integrate the types of methods employed by the Swamp Fox and Col. Mosby. This force would combine these principles with new techniques of airborne and guerrilla fighting.

Private First Class Edeleanu prints news bulletin on bulletin board outside Intelligence tent of Kyaukpyu Camp, the day before Office of Strategic Services (OSS), AFU, departure via convoy for Rangoon. Detachment 101, Ramree Island, Burma. *National Archive*

They were know as Shadow Warriors. Their organization would become known as the Office of Strategic Service, or OSS.

Prior to the United States becoming involved in World War II, President Franklin D. Roosevelt realized the need for the collection of intelligence and special operation capabilities. He authorized creation of the Office of the Coordinator of Information (COI), formed under the leadership of William "Wild Bill" Donovan in 1941. The COI

flourished, establishing operations sites in England, North Africa, India, Burma, and China.

When the United States entered World War II in December 1941, the COI agency was renamed the Office of Strategic Services. The OSS was instrumental in gathering intelligence and conducting sabotage raids in occupied Europe. It also worked with the French resistance fighting against the Nazis.

In April of 1942, Detachment 101 of the OSS was activated for service in Burma. Under the command of General "Vinegar Joe" Stillwell, this unit conducted operations behind the Japanese line in Burma. Detachment 101 consisted of nearly 11,000 Kachin tribesmen. Starting from scratch, these guerrillas were responsible for killing 10,000 Japanese, while losing only 206 of their own.

On 23 December 1942, the Joint Chiefs of Staff authorized the formation of multi-national Operation Groups (OGs), for which Donovan had been the principal advocate. The OGs were French, Greek, German, Italian, Norwegian, and Yugoslavian. These units included specially selected, trained, and disciplined U.S. Army soldiers who were proficient in conducting operations behind enemy lines. An Operation Group comprised 30 enlisted men and three officers, further split into two 15-man sections. OGs were the forerunners of the Operational Detachments-Alpha (ODAs), or A-teams, of today's Special Forces.

The mission of the OGs was to infiltrate by parachute or sometimes by sea into enemy territory. There they would meet up with existing guerrilla forces and support them in conducting unconventional warfare. Like current ODAs, the OGs were self-sufficient and had the ability to train and coordinate guerrilla operations. Such operations included, but were not limited to, direct sabotage, rescue of downed Allied pilots, and collection of intelligence. Although efforts were made to coordinate their action with the

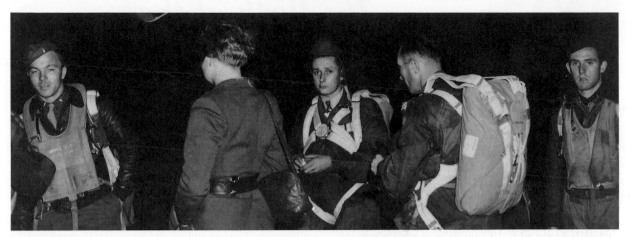

OSS Jedburgh team members prepare to board a B-24 bomber for their parachute drop behind German lines. Operating primarily at night, B-24s of the 801st Bombardment Group, known as the Carpetbaggers, supported missions the same as today's Combat Talons—penetrate enemy airspace and infiltrate special operations teams. *National Archive*

Resistance, the OGs could, and did, conduct raids and operations without any partisan support.

In the early part of 1944, in preparation of the D-Day invasion of France, the OSS began the creation of the first of the Jedburgh Teams, which eventually numbered 96. The name Jedburgh came from the area of Scotland where the Scots carried on a guerrilla war against the British invaders in the twelfth century.

The typical Jedburgh Team consisted of three men—two officers and one enlisted radio operator. These individuals were trained in demolitions, weapons, knife fighting, hand-to-hand combat, infiltration and exfiltration techniques, small units tactics, survival, and a multitude of other unconventional warfare skills to assure them success in their missions behind the German lines.

The mission of the Jedburgh Teams was to infiltrate, via parachute primarily, occupied France, Belgium, and Holland prior to the D-Day invasion. There they would organize guerrillas and conduct unconventional warfare against the Nazis, providing the resistance fighters with supplies and weapons. Operations began on D-Day to ambush German convoys, disrupt communications, destroy railways, bridges, and roadways and to delay enemy reinforcements from reaching the beachhead at Normandy.

At the conclusion of World War II, President Harry S. Truman deactivated the OSS, yet its legacy lives on today. The intelligence branch of the service is considered the father of the current Central Intelligence Agency (CIA), formed in September 1947. The first directors of the agency were former OSS veterans.

Special Forces thus drew inspiration and tactics from many sources throughout U.S. history and before our nation was formed. With each new conflict, the leaders of unconventional warfare drew on the proven techniques of the past, and added to them with resources and techniques of the time. World War II provided a pressing international stage on which to hone unconventional warfare techniques, and the lessons learned in that conflict have been extended and refined to the present day.

CHAPTER 2

The Birth of the U.S. Army Special Forces

Two OSS operatives, Col. Aaron Bank and Col. Russell Volckmann, remained in service with the U.S. Army. These two officers had been assigned to the Army Psychological Warfare Staff at the end of World War II, commanded by Brigadier General Robert McClure. Gen. McClure had been the director of information in the U.S.-occupied area of West Germany. A strong advocate of psychological warfare, he would take command of the Office of the Chief of Psychological Warfare (OCPW) on 15 January 1950. The OCPW was divided into three branches, PsyWar, covert deception, and Special Operations.

Working for the OCPW, Cols. Bank and Volckmann developed plans for organizing and training a special operations unit. They worked diligently to convince the Army Chiefs that the post–World War II world held numerous sites of potential conflict that would not be open to conventional warfare, but were prime targets for unconventional warfare tactics and guerrilla fighting. One such area was Eastern Europe, now occupied and dominated by the Soviets. Intelligence indicated that a substantial potential for guerrilla and covert Unconventional Warfare (UW) operations existed in the area.

Special operations units as envisioned by the two colonels, and Banks in particular, would be a force multiplier. Based on the OSS Jedburgh Teams, with striking similarities to today's Special Forces A-Detachments, these small teams could operate behind the enemy's lines and raise havoc and confusion within its ranks. It would be possible for a handful of men to effectively hamper, disrupt, and paralyze a much larger conventional force, e.g., the Soviets.

This was daring and innovative thinking that went against the grain of traditional, conventional concepts. However bold the idea, by 1952 the U.S. Army was at last ready to commence a new era of unconventional warfare.

The new organization would be referred to as "Special Forces," a name derived from the OGs fielded by the OSS in 1944. The Army allocated

The original beret crest of the U.S. Army Special Forces—the Trojan Horse centered in a shield with a lightning bolt in the background, resting on a pair of airborne wings. This crest can still be seen in use today at the headquarters of the 10th Special Forces Group (Airborne) at Fort Carson, Colorado, and in Germany.

2,300 personnel slots for the unit and assigned it to Fort Bragg, North Carolina.

In the spring of 1952, Col. Bank headed to Fort Bragg to choose the location for a Psychological Warfare/Special Forces Center. The area he selected is still the home of Special Forces, located at the corner of Reilly Road and Ardennes. This area was, and remains to this day, Smoke Bomb Hill. Although a remote location at Fort Bragg in 1952, within a decade it would become one of the busiest areas in the U.S. Army.

At this time Col. Bank began bringing together selected officers and NCOs who would serve as the nucleus of the new organization. These men would act as the training cadre to fill in the ranks of the fledgling unit. Col. Bank did

The father of the U.S. Army Special Forces, Colonel Aaron Bank. He was the first Special Forces Commander, commanding the 10th Special Forces Group (Airborne) as it was organized in June 1952 at Smoke Bomb Hill, Ft. Bragg, North Carolina. *JFK Special Warfare Museum*

not want any inexperienced soldiers; from the inception of Special Forces, only the best troops were sought, and Banks got them. Among the ranks assembled in the newly formed organization were former OSS officers, airborne troops, Ranger troops, and combat veterans from World War II and Korea.

The individuals who volunteered for service with the newly formed Special Forces were unique, highly motivated men looking for new challenges—the tougher the better! Virtually all the soldiers were fluent in at least two languages, had the minimum rank of sergeant and were trained in infantry and airborne skills. They were all volunteers who were willing to work behind enemy lines. They further agreed to operate in civilian

When first organized in 1952, members of the Special Forces wore the Glider and Parachute airborne patch. Subsequently, it would be replaced with the Arrowhead patch, which is the current shoulder patch of the SF soldiers.

clothes as necessary. This in itself would be dangerous, since soldiers in civilian clothes were no longer protected under the Geneva Convention and most likely would be executed if captured.

But the men who volunteered did not worry about the risks. Mr. Joe Lupyak SF-CSM (ret.) relates that "most of the early SF troops were foreigners." Indeed, many of the early troopers were from Eastern Europe, and had lived through their share of communist tyranny and Nazi rule. They had fled to America after the end of World War II under the provisions of the Lodge Bill, a law that allowed immigrants from politically persecuted countries to become U.S. citizens by serving in the United States armed forces.

Because of their backgrounds and motivation, the men of the first Special Forces organization were ideally suited for guerrilla operations in Eastern Europe. This was precisely the geographical area Bank had in mind when he designed the

Members of the 10th Special Forces Group (Airborne) take a break in the Bavarian mountainside. A number of the early SF soldiers were not from the United States. They joined under the Lodge Bill, a legislative act designed to allow immigrants from politically persecuted countries to become U.S. citizens by serving in the U.S. armed forces. The soldier on the left is armed with a Czechoslovakian submachine gun. *JFK Special Warfare Museum*

Members of the 10th Special Forces Group (Airborne) during mountain training, seen here wearing the forbidden green berets. In the early years the beret was often worn in the field, but rarely, if ever, worn in garrison. Note the glider and parachute shoulder patch worn by the original SF units. *JFK Special Warfare Museum*

group. Not only were they fluent with the language of the targeted areas, they were also familiar with the local customs, political sentiments, police, and industrial structure, as well as the overall geography.

After months of concentrated preparation, the new unit was ready. On 19 June 1952, the 10th Special Forces Group (Airborne) was activated, under the command of Col. Aaron Bank. On the day of its activation, the 10th SFG (A) had a total complement of ten soldiers—Col. Bank, one warrant officer, and eight enlisted men. This fledgling organization would soon flourish into a formidable force.

Within months of its activation, hundreds of the first volunteers reported to Smoke Bomb Hill as they completed the initial phase of their Special Forces training. As the group grew in size, it was divided into a compilation of three types of detachments or teams: A-teams, B-Teams, and C-Teams.

Students from the Special Warfare Center go through their final exercises in the National Forest area near Ft. Bragg, North Carolina. This exercise, known as Robin Sage, will pit the newly trained SF students against a larger conventional "enemy" force. Uniform of the day is "guerrilla casual" so they can blend in with the locals. *JFK Special Warfare Museum*

The basic operational unit of Special Forces was the A-detachment or A-team. The A-team consisted of twelve men—two officers and ten enlisted men—and was commanded by a captain. The A-team was the core of the new Special Forces. They were the soldiers who would be on the ground deep inside enemy territory. Their job was to make contact with the local resistance leaders and develop the indigenous population into a cohesive guerrilla force. The A-team had two operations and intelligence sergeants, two medical sergeants, two communications sergeants, two weapons sergeants, and two demolition/engineer sergeants. This configuration would allow the A-team to operate in two six-man teams or "split A-teams" if necessary. It was standard operating procedure that

each member of the A-team was crossed-trained in the SF skills. A-team soldiers were highly trained in unconventional warfare and spoke at least one foreign language. To this day the A-team remains the basis of Special Forces operations.

The functions of the B- and C-teams were more organizational. B-teams coordinated the actions of numerous A-teams assigned to specific areas in a designated country. C-teams were at the top of the Special Forces hierarchy. They worked with top leaders of indigenous guerrilla movements, and provided overall guidance to other SF teams in the area.

As soon as the 10th group was large enough, Banks started training his soldiers in the most advanced unconventional warfare techniques. The initial mission of the 10th Special Forces Group was to infiltrate designated areas of enemy territory by land, sea, or air and establish and train indigenous forces to conduct Special Forces operations, with an emphasis on guerrilla warfare. There were also secondary missions, including deep-penetration raids, intelligence-gathering assignments, and counter-insurgency operations. Special Forces operations demanded a commitment to professionalism and excellence unparalleled in the history of America's military, but the men of the 10th Special Forces Group (Airborne) were up to the challenge.

Like today's Special Forces soldier, the men under Col. Banks' newly formed organization were Airborne qualified and many of them had undergone Ranger training as well. Familiar with tough training, volunteers for Special Forces quickly realized this was not a mere review of Ranger tactics. As Banks put the men through their paces, they would learn many more skills, undergo more intense training, practice different mission profiles, and master more complex operations.

The Ranger units of World War II and the Korean War had been created to perform as shock troops and carry out light infantry raids—to hit and run and wait for follow-on forces. Special Forces troops, by contrast, were expected to remain behind enemy lines for months on end, perhaps even years. They would be self-sufficient experts in survival, capable of living off the land. And they would speak the language of the indigenous populace in their area of operation.

The Special Forces soldier would learn all of these skills and many more. Operating as a full Special Forces Group for less than 18 months, the men of the 10th Special Forces demonstrated to the Army that they were masters of these unconventional and very useful skills.

With the political climate heating up in East Germany, half of the 10th Special Forces Group was re-deployed on 11 November 1953 to Bad Tolz, West Germany. These A-teams would be on call to provide support to any resistance movements, if necessary, in Soviet-occupied Europe. The other half of the group would remain at Fort Bragg and was redesignated the 77th Special Forces Group. This split was significant, as it demonstrated that Special Forces had established itself as a vital unit of the U.S. Army.

During the balance of the 1950s, Special Forces would continue to grow, slowly but consistently, into a formidable organization. Special Forces was surveying its interest in the Far East, moving beyond their previous European focus. In April 1956 the 14th Special Forces Detachment (Area) (Airborne) was secretly activated at Fort Bragg; two months later they would deploy to Hawaii, and subsequently to Thailand, Taiwan, and Vietnam.

This detachment of 16 SF soldiers taken from the 77th SFG was tasked with the mission of leading Asian resistance against any communist thrust into Indo-China, Malaya, South Korea, and the surrounding area. Operations in Korea were not new to Special Forces personnel. Near the end of 1952, Special Forces troops had been operating behind enemy lines and had been deployed on classified missions. Special Forces soldiers assisted anti-communist guerrillas who had joined the United Nation Partisan Forces-Korea or UNPFK. These guerrillas were often referred to as "donkeys," from the Korean word for liberty, dong-il. The guerrillas, operating from small islands off the Korean coast, would conduct raids, rescue downed airmen, provide gunnery spotting, and maintain electronic facilities. This would be the first time that U.S. Army Special Forces would operate with guerrilla troops behind enemy lines.

Shortly after the activation of the 14th SFOD, three additional operational detachments, the 12th, 13th, and 16th, were designated for service in Asia and the Pacific. These three SFOD were

President Kennedy speaks with Brigadier General William P. Yarborough at Fort Bragg, 12 October 1961. President Kennedy would later comment that the green beret was "a symbol of excellence, a badge of courage, a mark of distinction in the fight for freedom." *JFK Library*

eventually combined into the 8231st Army Special Operations Detachment. On 17 June 1957 the 14th and 8231st united to form the 1st Special Forces Group (Airborne) based out of Okinawa and responsible for the Far Eastern area of operation. In the summer of 1959, Special Forces training teams would be inserted covertly into Laos to train soldiers of the Royal Lao Army. These SF teams were designated "White Star" mobile training teams, or MTT. Working under the direction of the Central Intelligence Agency (CIA), the Special Forces MTTs were also used to train Meo tribesmen as a guerrilla force.

By 1961 there were three active Special Forces groups securely established in the U.S. Army—the 1st Special Forces Group (Airborne), the 7th Special Forces Group (Airborne) (re-designated from the 77th on 6 June 1960), and the original 10th Special Forces Group (Airborne).

The Cold War produced increased demand for unconventional tactics and soldiers. The Special Forces were in Berlin when the Berlin wall was erected. Special Forces personnel would conduct cross-border operations, some of these missions still classified today. These soldiers were assigned to a unit known simply as detachment "A." When in garrison, they would not wear the SF patches or berets; they would blend in with other conventional troops wearing the Berlin brigade patch. As their Office of Strategic Services (OSS) predecessors, when these soldiers would go out to roam around Germany, they would do so in civilian clothes. The clothes they wore, the shoes on their feet, their rucksacks, and even their underwear were of German origin. There would be nothing to trace them to the United States if they were compromised.

Other missions given to the Special Forces during this time included training Cuban expatriates. Special Forces teams were sent to Guatemala to train soldiers for the possible invasion of Cuba again in October of 1962 during the Cuban Missile Crisis, when the Soviets placed offensive nuclear missiles in Cuba. The U.S. military was put on full alert, including Special Forces teams placed on standby, should the call for their insertion be sent.

If Col. Aaron Bank was the father of the Special Forces, then President John F. Kennedy was to become their godfather. President Kennedy, a military scholar with more than a mere interest in counterinsurgency, recognized the need for a counter-guerrilla force. He referred to this as "another type of war, new in its intensity, ancient in its origins—war by guerrillas, subversives, insurgents, assassins; war by ambush instead of by combat; by infiltration instead of aggression, seeking victory by eroding and exhausting the enemy instead of engaging him." This, he continued, would require "a whole new kind of strategy, a wholly different kind of force."

During his visit to Ft. Bragg in 1961, President Kennedy found such a force as he reviewed the men of the U.S. Army Special Forces. These dedicated soldiers were what the President was looking for to thwart the spreading threat of communist insurgents around the world. President Kennedy also liked the green beret headgear. These men had a special mission; it was only fitting they have a special symbol to set that mission apart. As the ranks of the Special Forces grew, the green beret became synonymous with Special Forces.

With the support of the President, the Special Forces grew, and additional SF groups were formed. On 21 September 1961, the 5th Special Forces Group (Airborne) was activated, followed by the 8th SFG(A) on 1 April 1963, the 6th SFG(A) on 1 May 1963, and finally the 3rd SFG(A) on 5 December 1963. Members of the Special Forces would also find themselves in Army Reserve and National Guard units with the formation of the 11th and 12th SFG(A)—Reserve and 19th and 20th SFG(A)—National Guard, in 1966.

Nineteen-sixty-three would see the death of the U.S. Army Special Forces' greatest proponent, President John F. Kennedy. He had given them a

On 29 May 1965, the United States Army John F. Kennedy Center for Special Warfare was dedicated. The ceremony was held in front of the first completed building of the Center, John F. Kennedy Hall. John F. Kennedy Hall would be a hub of activity for Special Forces operations during the Vietnam War.

"Bronze Bruce" stands as a memorial to the Special Forces soldier. Depicted as a Sergeant First Class, he is armed with an M16 rifle signifying his readiness to do battle. Yet his other hand is open and outstretched, indicating his willingness to help and provide comfort.

mission, had given them the "green beret," and had set a course for the Special Forces soldier. On 29 May 1965, the date that would have been the president's 48th birthday, the United States Army John F. Kennedy Center for Special Warfare was dedicated. The ceremony was held in front of the first completed building of the Center, John F. Kennedy Hall.

The mission of the Special Warfare Center was to instruct selected U.S. military personnel, civilians, and eligible foreign offices; develop tactics and techniques for the Special Forces soldier in the field—e.g., infiltration methods, target analysis, operations and intelligence, communications, weapons, medical and engineering; prepare training documents in support of instructional programs and special unit training; coordinate with other armed forces and civilian agencies and support training activities of the U.S. Continental Army Command, USCONARC.

Special Warfare was defined at this time as the application of three associated activities as carried out by highly trained soldiers to achieve the nation's objective, whether in cold, limited, or general war. Those three areas were Counterinsurgency Operations, Unconventional Warfare, and Psychological Operations.

Counterinsurgency Operations would include any and all military, political, and economic actions taken to eliminate subversive insurgency. Subversive insurgency, e.g., wars of liberation, had received increased support by the communists as a primary course of action to extend communist control. Counterinsurgency Operations required the integration and coordination of all military and non-military resources to achieve the necessary results.

Unconventional Warfare encompassed guerrilla warfare, evasion and escape, and sabotage against hostile forces. UW operations would be conducted within enemy territory or enemy-controlled areas by establishing, training, and supporting the indigenous personnel in carrying out these missions.

Psychological Operations included PsyWar (psychological warfare) and covered the political, military, economic, and ideological actions necessary to create in enemy, neutral, or friendly forces the emotions, attitudes, or behaviors to support the national objectives.

Throughout the early 1960s soldiers of the Special Forces participated in more than six major exercises and more than 74 smaller FTXs (Field Training Exercises) ranging from Exercise Polar Strike in Alaska to Quick Kick VII conducted in the Caribbean. Soldiers from SF groups would be included in counter-guerrilla and counterinsurgency warfare training with assorted conventional units located in the continental United States.

Many Special Forces soldiers with distinct capabilities as teachers were assigned to Army Special Action Forces (SAF). These units would be tasked with civil affairs, engineer, intelligence, military police, and psychological operations units. Five such units were active: one for Asia, one for Latin America, one for Europe, and two for Africa and the Middle East. SAF instruction in medicine, sanitation, agricultural techniques, local government administrations, communications, and basic commerce was a direct deterrent to the spread of communism.

Simultaneous with these other activities, the Special Forces soldiers and groups constantly prepared for the UW task of infiltrating deep into enemy-controlled territory to contact, organize, train, equip, and advise the local partisans for guerrilla warfare against a common enemy.

During this time Special Forces soldiers were sent all over the globe in MTT. In 1965, for example, 25 MTT were deployed to 14 different countries. These countries included Argentina, Bolivia, Brazil, Ethiopia, Iran, Iraq, Jordan, Mali, Nepal, Nigeria, Pakistan, Peru, the Philippines, and the Republic of the Congo.

The missions of these teams varied by country, but would include aerial delivery methods, communications, engineering/demolition, language interpretation, medical instruction, and other tactical training. Lt. General William P. Yarborough called the Special Forces soldiers "the finest representatives that the United States Army has ever had." These MTT missions assisting friendly foreign countries expanded the role of the SF soldier from unconventional warfare and counterinsurgency to one of today's important SF functions, Foreign Internal Defense.

With the growing success of its teams and their missions, the Special Forces had soldiers who had seen action all over the world. Not all of the missions were benign in nature. While the public's and military's primary attention was directed to the area of Southeast Asia, SF teams were quite active in Latin America. Members of the 8th Special Forces Group (Airborne) operating out of Fort Guick, in the Panama Canal Zone, were involved in operations against communist-backed guerrillas in Latin America. Special Forces soldiers would be involved in the pursuit and capture of Ernesto "Che" Guevara, a known Cuban revolutionary in the mountainous terrain in the country of Bolivia in 1968.

Special Forces was originally created to provide an unconventional warfare force in the event of Soviet aggression in Europe. It would not be the massing of Soviet armor funneling through the Fulda Gap, however, that would give Special Forces the action they were trained to carry out. The small wars of liberation referred to by President Kennedy would be where the Special Forces would come of age. They were the watershed for soldiers of the green beret.

CHAPTER 3

Baptism by Fire: Vietnam

While many people believe America's involvement in Vietnam was initiated by President Kennedy, it was actually President Dwight D. Eisenhower who first committed U.S. troops to southeast Asia. The French debacle at Dien Bien Phu in 1954 left a void in the region, opening it to the spread of communism.

Special Forces soldiers were among the first U.S. advisers sent to the Republic of Vietnam. Here members of the 5th Special Forces Group (Airborne) are armed with M1 Garand rifles, carbines, and BARs (Browning Automatic Rifles) and wear an assortment of uniforms, from early issue jungle fatigues to the "duck hunter" camouflage. Note the SF Captain, (kneeling, left) is holding a newly issued AR-15 rifle, the predecessor to the M-16. *U.S. Army Photo*

At this time President Eisenhower promised direct aid to the government of South Vietnam. In 1957 the first U.S. Army Special Forces soldiers actually arrived in Vietnam. That summer members of the 1st SFG(A) would train members of the Vietnamese Army at the Commando Training Center located at Nha Trang. This began the official involvement of U.S. Army Special Forces in Vietnam, which would last for 14 years until their withdrawal in February 1971.

During the time period of 1959–1960, South Vietnamese insurgents referred to as Viet Cong (Vietnamese communists) were growing in numbers and in power. The VC, as they came to be called, would move through villages spreading terror, torture, and destruction among the people. Thirty Special Forces soldiers were sent to South Vietnam in May 1960 to set up a training program for the army of Vietnam. It was on 21 September 1961 that the new president, John F. Kennedy, made good his inaugural address, "we shall support any friend, oppose any foe." His deep concern over the communist insurgents in South Vietnam drew the president to the Special Forces and their capability. The 5th Special Forces Group, 1st Special Forces, were made responsible for conduct of all SF missions in Vietnam.

To the average American citizen, places such as Nam Dong, Plei Mei, Kontum, Lang Vei, Dak To, and Bu Brang were unknown locations on a map. To the men of the Special Forces they were home, fortresses where they took a stand for freedom. These names meant camps where SF soldiers labored to build a future for liberty, bunkers where they spilled their blood, and a handful of dirt where some gave the ultimate sacrifice for what they believed in: "De Oppresso Liber." (SF motto: To Free the Oppressed.)

In the early part of U.S. involvement in Vietnam, Special Forces soldiers carried out missions to train a guerrilla force. According to intelligence from the CIA, the SF teams were deployed to the central highlands of South Vietnam to begin training the Montagnards (a French term defined as "mountain people"). The Montagnards numbered more than 500,000 in South Vietnam and came from approximately 20 different tribes. The agency had recognized the Montagnards as a possible ally in the war against the communists.

Special Forces began a program with mountain people that would become known as CIDG, or Civilian Irregular Defense Group. The organization and training of this paramilitary group became the primary mission for Special Forces in Vietnam. From 1961 to 1965 more than eight CIDG camps were built in the isolated countryside of South Vietnam. Each of these outposts was self-contained and manned by a CIDG Strike Force, a complement of South Vietnamese Special Forces and a U.S. Special Forces A-team. The primary role of the A-detachments took a turn from their origins in 1952. Instead of training a guerrilla force to interdict conventional army troops, they were now training indigenous tribesmen to conduct actions against other guerrillas, the Viet Cong.

Over the course of the war more than 250 outposts of A-Camps would be established throughout South Vietnam. Scattered along the Laos and Cambodian boarders, these strategically located outposts of freedom would become a considerable thorn in the side of the Viet Cong and later the North Vietnamese Army.

One such camp was Nam Dong, commanded by SF Captain Roger H. Donlon. Located some 32 miles west of Da Nang, the camp was distinctly in enemy territory. Established 15 miles from the Laotian border, it was placed strategically to inter-

"Green Beret" Staff Sergeant Arthur Fletcher assisted two members of the Vietnamese Special Forces in the repair of a 30-caliber machine gun. *U.S. Army Photo*

dict and harass the VC coming down the Ho Chi Minh from the North. Nam Dong was not like any other A-Camp design the SF soldiers had seen at Ft. Bragg—e.g., Plei Mei was triangular, Dak To circular, Lang Vei a diamond, and so on. This plot of real estate measured approximately 80 yards by 120 yards, looking more like a West Virginia ham than a formidable fortress. Beyond the camp perimeter was another area 350 yards long and 250 yards wide. Here is where the Vietnamese strike force lived, in about a dozen hootches. In addition to the "strikers," there was a contingent of 60 Nungs. (The Nungs were ethnic Chinese mercenaries who fought bravely, and were dedicated to the Special Forces soldiers they fought alongside.) Just beyond the outer fence line there lay a jungle airstrip, courtesy of the U.S. Navy Seabees.

Approximately 5,000 Katu tribesmen live in the area of the Nam Dong Valley. The SF Camp would provide them with medical attention and protection, and hopefully be a source of aggravation for the VC. The team medical specialists, Sgt. Thomas L. Gregg and Sgt. Terrance D. Terrin, would become the "popular" members of the team with the locals, as oftentime happened among the camps.

Nam Dong would be home for the Special Forces soldiers of A-726 (A-team-7th SFG(A)Team #26). What team A-726 did not know was that this civic action mission would turn into a life-or-death battle before they would leave.

At 0226 Monday 6 July 1964, the VC began their attack of Camp Nam Dong. Mortar rounds, grenades, and small arms fire erupted from every direction. The Special Forces soldiers were surrounded. SSG Keith Daniels, shaken out of bed by the first explosion, was now on the camp's radio. He made contact with Da Nang and requested a flare ship and air strike. Hearing explosions coming closer to his position, he knew the communications shed was next. He grabbed his AR-15 and hit the door. Just as he left, the building exploded behind him.

By now the Nungs and South Vietnamese had moved to their fighting positions, and the SF were manning the mortar pits. A typical mortar pit was approximately eight feet around, with sandbags stacked around the edge to provide some protection from small arms fire and flying fragments. Located at the rear of the pit was a cement bunker housing 300 rounds of assorted ammunition for the tube—high explosive (HE) and white phosphorous, either 60mm or 81mm, accordingly.

President Kennedy had referred to the green beret as a "symbol of excellence, a badge of courage, a mark of distinction in the fight for freedom." The men of team A-726 put their training and experience to work that morning. From bunkers, mortar pits, or behind debris piles, the Special Forces soldiers were returning fire

By the spring of 1970, more than 350 U.S. pilots had been captured and held in prison camps in North Vietnam. These pilots and aircrews were exposed to appalling living conditions and subjected to frequent beatings and torture. The majority of American captives in the North were not even allowed contact with other prisoners or the outside world.

In May of 1970, reconnaissance photographs revealed the existence of two prison camps west of Hanoi. At Son Tay, one of the recce photos showed a large letter "K" drawn in the dirt. This was a code for "come get us."

Brigadier General Donald D. Blackburn, who had trained Filipino guerrillas during World War II, recommended that a small hand-picked group of Special Forces volunteers be assembled to mount a rescue operation to liberate these prisoners. For this operation, he choose Lt. Colonel Arthur D. "Bull" Simons to lead the force.

Since the prison compound was located more than 20 miles west of Hanoi, operation planners believed Son Tay was isolated enough to enable a small group to land, rescue the prisoners, and withdraw. A full-scale replica of the prison compound was constructed at Eglin Air Force Base, Florida. Here a select group of Special Forces soldiers trained at night for the mission. The mock compound was dismantled during the day to avoid detection by Soviet satellites. A model of the camp was built that would allow the raiders to view the camp under various light to duplicate moonlight, flares, night vision, and so on. The replica was named "Barbara." To be successful, the troops needed to be prepared, yet time was running out. Evidence, although inconclusive, showed that Son Tay may have been empty.

On 18 November 1970 Col. Simons moved his raiders to Takhli, Thailand, to begin staging for the mission. Only Col. Simons and three others knew what the final mission would be. Five hours before takeoff, 20 November, Col. Simons informed his force of 59 men, "We are going to rescue 70 American prisoners of war, maybe more, from a camp called Son Tay. This is something American prisoners have a right to expect from their fellow soldiers. The target is 23 miles west of Hanoi." As Col. Simons left the room the solders broke into applause.

Approximately 0215, Hanoi time, on 21 November 1970, the raid began. An Air Force C-130 flare ship illuminated the area with flares, and the HH-53 began firing on the guard towers with its twin Gatling guns. The U.S. Navy also provided diversionary fire. The raiders now had less than 30 minutes to land and complete their mission before they would have to face North Vietnamese reinforcements. The only problem was, the helicopter mistakenly set down at another site. Instead of being just outside the prison compound, the support group was some 400 meters away at what was referred to as a 'secondary school' on the maps. This building was a barracks that housed Chinese and Soviet advisers and a large number of NVA troops. The raiders took this force under fire and eliminated them from reinforcing the prison.

After this brief encounter, Col. Simons and the support group re-loaded his HH-53 and moved to the prison compound. Nine minutes into the raid, Col. Simons was outside the prison wall. There, he and the support element augmented the assault and security elements and eliminated approximately 60 guards. However, as they searched from building to building the hard facts begin to sink in, there were no American prisoners. There were no prisoners whatsoever. The Son Tay raid ended after 27 minutes and the raiders were once again airborne. The force had not lost a single man, and al-

The Son Tay Raid Patch

though there were no prisoners to rescue, the planning and execution itself were flawless. To this day the Son Tay raid is often referred to as a "textbook" mission.

"Outpost of Freedom." This aerial photo shows a good overview of an SF camp. Scattered throughout South Vietnam, these fighting camps would serve as bases of operations against the Viet Cong and later the North Vietnamese Army troops. Numerous layouts and plans were tried; this plan, referred to as a star pattern, was one of the later designs. Each tip of the star is a fighting bunker, and as you move in toward the core of the camp you can see additional motor pits or machine gun emplacements. This also is where the "Green Berets" would set up their Tactical Operations Center. *JFK Special Warfare Museum*

toward the rushing horde of VC guerrillas. As the courageous troops fought to defend their camp, the VC kept coming. Two reinforced VC battalions, more than 800 guerrillas, had managed to encircle the camp. They had already penetrated the outer perimeter and were now bearing down on team A-726.

After five hours of intense fighting, the defenders of the camp successfully thwarted the VC attack. Camp Nam Dong had survived, but not without a cost: 55 of the camp's defenders had been killed. Among them, MSgt. Gabriel R. Alamo and Sgt. John Houston, members of A-726, and

an Australian Warrant Officer, Kevin Conway. The body count showed that more than 200 VC had died in the failed attack.

On 5 December 1964, President Lyndon B. Johnson awarded the Medal of Honor to Captain Roger Donlon, who had particularly distinguished himself. The text of the citation explains that "Captain Roger C. Donlon, 7th Special Forces Group (Airborne), 1st Special Forces, distinguished himself on 6 July 1964, while commanding Special Forces Detachment A-726 at Nam Dong, republic of Vietnam. On 6 July, the camp was assaulted in a pre-dawn attack by a reinforced Viet

Cong battalion. During the violent five-hour battle, resulting in numerous causalities on both sides, Captain Donlon directed the overall defense of the camp. He swiftly marshaled his forces and ordered the removal of needed ammunition from a blazing building hit by the initial assault. He then dashed through a hail of small arms and exploding hand grenade fire to a breach of the main gate where he detected and annihilated an enemy three-man demolition team. Exposed to an intense attack and sustaining a severe stomach wound, he succeeded in reaching the 60mm mortar pit. Discovering most of the men in the gun pit were wounded, Captain Donlon disregarding his own injury, risked his own life by remaining in the pit and returning the enemy fire, allowing

Captain Roger H. Donlon returns to the Special Forces camp at Nam Dong, where he was the Officer in Charge when the camp was attacked by the Viet Cong on 6 July 1964 by a force estimated to be of battalion size. He inspects what is left of the mess hall. Captain Donlon was the first soldier to be awarded the Medal of Honor during the Vietnam War. By the end of the conflict, Special Forces soldiers would bring home 17 Medals of Honor, our nation's highest award for gallantry above and beyond the call of duty. *National Archive*

the men to withdraw. While dragging his team sergeant out of the gun pit, an enemy mortar round exploded, hitting Captain Donlon's left shoulder. Suffering from multiple wounds, he carried the 60mm mortar to a new location 30 meters away where he found another three wounded defenders. After administering first aid and encouragement to these men, he left the weapon with them and then raced toward another location, retrieving a 57mm recoilless rifle. With great courage under fire, he returned to the abandoned gun pit, evacuated ammunition for the weapons and crawling and dragging back the urgently needed ammunition, received a third wound on his leg. Despite his critical condition, he crawled 175 meters to an 81mm mortar position and began directing firing operations, which protected the east sector of the camp. Until daylight brought defeat of the enemy forces, Captain Donlon moved from position to position around the beleaguered perimeter, hurling grenades at the enemy and inspiring his men to superhuman effort. Captain Donlon's conspicuous gallantry, extraordinary heroism and intrepidity at the risk

Special Forces with I Field Force Vietnam, Ban Me Thout. Assisted by U.S. Special Forces and indigenous personnel, the people of Buen Tor 1, some 10 miles south of Ban Me Thuot, evacuated their former homes. *U.S. Army Photo*

of his life above and beyond the call are in the highest tradition of the military service, reflecting the utmost credit upon himself, the Special Forces and the United States Army."

At the award ceremony, Captain Donlon said the award belonged to the entire team—to the valiant men of Special Forces Detachment A-726.

This was the first Medal of Honor to be awarded in the Vietnam war, but it would not be the last earned by the Special Forces. Sixteen of the nation's highest award, the MOH, would go to Special Forces soldiers: SFC Eugene Ashley, Jr.*, Detachment A-101, 5th SFG(A)—Lang Vei; Sgt. Gary B. Beikirch, Detachment B-24, 5th SFG(A)— Dak Seang; SSgt. Ray P. Benavidez, Detachment ·B-56, 5th SFG(A)—Loc Ninh; SFC William M. Bryant*, 5th SFG(A)—Long Khanh Province; Sgt. Brian L. Buker*, Detachment B-55, 5th SFG(A)— Chau Doc Province; SSgt. Jon R. Cavaiani—U.S. Army Vietnam Advisory Group; SSgt. Drew D. Dix—Chau Doc Province; 1st Lt. Loren D. Hagen*—U.S. Army Vietnam Advisory Group; SSgt. Charles E. Hosking, Jr.*, Detachment A-302, 5th SFG(A) Phuoc Long Province; SFC Robert L. Howard, 5th SFG(A); Specialist Fifth Class John J. Kedenburg*, Command and Control Detachment North, 5th SFG(A); SSgt. Franklin D. Miller, 5th SFG(A); 1st Lt. George K. Sissler*, 5th SFG(A); 1st Lt. Charles Q. Williams, 5th SFG(A)—Dong Xoai; Sgt. Gordon D. Yntema*, Detachment A-431, 5th SFG(A)—Cai Cai; SSgt. Fred W. Zabitosky, SOG.

The battle for Nam Dong was not an anomaly. In fact the Special Forces Camps were such a barb in the side of the VC that the communists would sacrifice thousands of their troops to try to dislodge a team or overrun a camp. Occasionally they did succeed, but only after the SF team extracted a heavy toll. If you go to a map of South Vietnam and pick a camp, there will be story for each one—Plei Mei in 1965, a battle so intense it would mark a major turn in U.S. involvement to the ground war in Vietnam; Lang Vei in 1968, where the communists had to employ Soviet-supplied PT-76 tanks in order to overrun the camp; Ben Het, where the NVA laid siege to the isolated post for two months, never taking it over; Dak To, Dak Pek, Dak Seang, Bu Brang, the list goes on. Strange names on a tactical map, hundreds of camps, and a thousand acts of heroism by Special Forces soldiers.

In addition to the tenacity of the SF teams located in these camps demonstrated, they had the versatility to employ various methods of turning the tide in their favor should the proverbial "hit the fan." The U.S. Air Force, Air Commandos flew AC-47 Gunships, "Spooky" and "Puff the Magic Dragon," that were often on call. TAC air, whether A-1E "Spads" or the fast movers, F-4 Phantoms, could be overhead in minutes. There were even times when B-52 bombers would rain down terror to break the assault on a camp in trouble. While all these sources provided outstanding assistance, the Special Forces also had an ace up their sleeves. Organic to the Special Forces, it was a group the camps called in when they were in danger of being overrun: the MIKE Force.

The MIKE Forces were Mobile Strike Forces. Each force consisted of three companies of soldiers, giving them a strength of 600 men. These units comprised elite CIDGs that would act as quick reaction forces to support the SF camps. Because of their loyalty and aggressiveness, Nungs were often well represented in the MIKE Forces. Highly trained in airborne and helicopter operations, the MIKE Forces could be called in to reinforce a camp and turn the tide in favor of the Special Forces soldiers on the ground.

Unlike other assets in theater, the MIKE Force was under direct control of the U.S. Special Forces and commanded by SF soldiers. Under the control of the "C" detachment commander, by 1968 there were five Mobile Strike Force Commands in Vietnam, numbering approximately 2,000 men per command. These forces were highly responsive and

(* *awarded posthumously*)

could be placed into action at a moment's notice. For this reason, members of the MIKE Force seldom had the luxury of sitting around garrison. They would return from an engagement often with only enough time to resupply and load up on the helicopters for the next run. The soldiers of the MIKE Force were the "cavalry" in Huey's, and many a besieged SF camp owes its survival to this group of courageous soldiers, both American and indigenous. By the end of 1966 the 5th Special Forces Group (Airborne) had an operational strength of 2,400 men, with strike forces numbering 33,400 indigenous troops and supported by 2,400 MIKE Force soldiers.

Special Forces soldiers leading indigenous troops were also employed at this time by the Central Intelligence Agency (CIA) to conduct reconnaissance operations. Reconnaissance teams, or RTs, usually consisted of two SF soldiers and four indigenous personnel. These early CIA-sponsored operations were referred to as PROJECT DELTA and filled Military Assistance Command Vietnam (MACV) intelligence requirements across the entire country. The capability of these small teams proved so valuable that subsequent recce missions were formed in the operations known as Projects, GAMMA, SIGMA, and OMEGA.

These small teams were extremely vulnerable to the larger communist forces they were sent to study. Helicopters were regularly called in to extract an RT from a "hot" (enemy engaged) landing zone (LZ). For the times when the helicopters could not land, the RT could be extracted with the use of the McGuire rig, named after Special Forces Sergeant Major Charles McGuire, who invented it. The McGuire rig was a simple rope 100 feet long with a canvas sling attached; it would be lowered to the ground from a hovering helicopter. The team member on the ground could quickly place himself in the sling and hold on, to be snatched from grasp of the enemy as the helicopter pulled him out. Four of these rigs could be fitted on a helicopter at one time.

In addition to providing special reconnaissance, 5th SFG(A) established the MACV Renaissance/Commando School in September 1966, located in Nha Trang, South Vietnam. Known as the "Recondo" School, this three-week course trained the indigenous forces in helicopter insertions and extractions techniques, survival, evasion and escape (E&E), communications, weapons (U.S. and enemy), intelligence gathering methods, and other subjects pertaining to Special Forces operations. Non-airborne soldiers would also receive parachute training. Members of U.S. Long Range Reconnaissance Patrols (LRRPs) and recon troop from Vietnam, Korea, and other allied countries also attended the Recondo School.

Because of the many successes of the CIDG program, in addition to the U.S. buildup of conventional troops in Vietnam during 1965–1966, the Special Forces–led CIDG units shifted to more offensive operations. In late 1966, Colonel Francis "Blackjack" Kelly, then commander of 5th SFG(A), presented the plan for the formation of the Mobile Guerrilla Force (MGF). Col. Kelly envisioned a company-size force that would operate in the same method as Merrill's Marauders operated in Burma during World War II.

The MGF was to be a small, self-contained unit; there would be no artillery support or reinforcements flown in to fill in for casualties. The only support that would be provided would come from a lone Forward Air Control aircraft. Resupply of the MGF would be done not by transport or helicopter but by fighter planes. In order not to compromise the troop's location, A-1E Skyraiders flown by the U.S. Air Commandos would drop napalm canisters, fitted with parachutes, filled with up 400 pounds of food, ammunition, and other supplies. The purpose of the MGF would be to drop in the middle of a known enemy's area of operation and create havoc. Col. Kelly was putting the VC on notice—SF was in town and they were going hunting! Hunting was good. The MGF

A captain from the 6th Special Forces Group (Airborne) goes over a mission plan with his A-team. Planning, rehearsing, and evaluating the mission are all part of the Special Forces operations. Every possible contingency they can think of is discussed and alternate measures developed. Very few things happen that have not been discussed in mission planning. Special Forces are successful because they "sweat the small stuff"! *U.S. Army Photo*

would be engaged in more than 50 battles, called in on countless air strikes against the enemy and involved in assaults on numerous company- and battalion-strength base camps. Mobile Guerrilla Force - Detachment A-303 was also responsible for recovering a highly sensitive "black box" from a U-2 aircraft operating with the SAC, Strategic Reconnaissance Wing, that had crashed.

The MIKE Force and MGF missions were highly successful. These units were large, however, and there was a need for a smaller, more covert unit. In February 1964 the commander of the MACV, General Paul D. Harkins, authorized the creation of

SOG. Officially the name stood for Studies and Observation Group; unofficially, and more exactly, it stood for Special Operations Group. While SOG did engage members of the other services, e.g., Navy SEALs, Air Commandos, and even USMC Force Recon, the majority of personnel came from the 5th Special Forces Group (Airborne).

The purpose of SOG was to conduct covert missions on "the other side of the fence." This meant the insertion of teams into North Vietnam, Laos (codename: Prairie Fire), and Cambodia (codename: Daniel Boone). SOG missions could include guerrilla warfare, direct action, sabotage, psychological operations, E&E nets, and other operations that are still classified. SOG was broken down into three operational areas: Command and Control North (CCN) with forward operating bases (FOB) located in the area of Hue and operating in North Vietnam and Laos; Command and Control Central (CCC), FOB in Kontum, operating in Laos and northeastern Cambodia; and Command and Control South (CCS), FOB located in Ban Me Thout and Quan Loi, operating in Cambodia.

A former SOG member reports that SOG teams would load M-16 cartridges with "pet," a high explosive. "We would wait until we got into a fire-fight with a [NVA] unit. We would begin our withdrawal and as we left, we'd drop magazines with these doctored rounds. They would be in for quite a surprise when they used them in their captured weapons." The "pet" round would blow up when the enemy tried to fire the weapon. A similar method was used in mortar rounds. A SOG team would infiltrate an enemy base camp and locate its ammunition supply. Instead of rigging it with explosives, the SOG members would plant these "special rounds" in the ammo boxes, and exfiltrate. Again, when the enemy would drop a round into the tube, it would explode. This had a marked psychological effect on the enemy concerning the quality of the ammunition they were receiving.

Although SOG forces regularly overcame overwhelming odds, not every mission dreamed up for them was realistic. One SOG veteran relates that as he was getting ready to go on R&R, he was called into the commander's office. There were rumors floating around that the Soviets had introduced tanks into the south and SOG wanted confirmation of this information. He had been chosen, since he had a background in armor and knew how to drive a tank. His mission was to be inserted "across the fence," locate one such tank, affix a white flag to its antenna and drive it back to friendly lines in the south. His eyes widened at the prospect of such a mission. He was also told that the tank was at a base camp deep inside enemy territory and had a regiment protecting it. This veteran continues, "Even some missions were just too wild for SOG. I said, thanks, then grabbed my bag and headed for R&R." (MACV/SOG would get its verification of the tanks some months later when 11 PT-76 tanks overran Lang Vie Special Forces camp.)

SOG teams took extremely high casualties. Often teams would have to run for their lives moving from one LZ to another hoping the Hueys could get them out in time. It was during the SOG missions that the STABO rig was developed. The name STABO was derived by the three SF soldiers from the Recondo School that developed the device: Major Robert Stevens, Captain John Knabb, and Sergeant First Class Clifford Roberts. For this device the soldier wore a specially designed web harness in place of his normal web gear. When the need for extraction came, the soldier would undo two straps from the back of the harness, secure them around his legs, then attach himself to the STABO yoke via carabiners at each shoulder. This harness differed from the McGuire rig in that it provided a more secure connection and allowed the user to keep his hands free to operate weapons as he flew through the air and out of harm's way.

Another method for extracting special operations personnel from the ground was the Fulton Surface-To-Air Recovery (STAR) system, known as "Skyhook." The STAR device consists of two containers that can be air-dropped to special forces units operating in a covert operation. Upon opening the canisters the soldiers on the ground would find a balloon, two helium inflation bottles, and an insulated flight suit and harness. When inflated, the balloon measured eight feet in diameter by 23 feet in length. Attached to the balloon would be a 500-foot nylon line equipped with marker flags for daylight extractions and strobe lights for nighttime operations. The individual to be extracted puts on the insulated flight suit and harness, hooks himself to the balloon's lines, and then sits facing the oncoming plane as the balloon is released and heads skyward.

A specially equipped MC-130 Combat Talon from the 90th Special Operations Squadron was also part of the Skyhook system. As the aircraft approached the recovery area, the yoke arms or "whiskers" were extended. These arms snagged the line in a locking device. The balloon would break away and the line would be fed into an attached hydraulic power winch in the rear of the

MACV-SOG (Military Assistance Command Vietnam–Studies and Observation Group) ran three AOs, or areas of operations. Command and Control North (CCN) operated in North Vietnam and Laos, Command and Control Central (CCC) operated in Laos and northeastern Cambodia, and Command and Control South (CCS) operated in Cambodia.

aircraft. The individual was then reeled into the ramp door. Along with personnel, the STAR system could also recover up to 500 pounds of equipment or material, if needed.

The soldiers of SOG were tasked with some of the most dangerous missions of the war. Reconnaissance teams became known as Spike Teams. Hatchet Teams, similar to a MIKE Force, would be ready to swoop in on any target the Spike Team exposed. The acronym for their missions said it all: SLAM—Search, Locate, Annihilate Mission. What more can you add? These were the types of missions assigned to SOG. Of the Medals of Honor given to SF soldiers in Vietnam, two went to SOG members.

Whatever the results of the Vietnam War, the men of the U.S. Army Special Forces emerged from the conflict with a permanent place in the history of the U.S. Army. They were highly adaptable in their fighting techniques. Introduced in the unconventional warfare role, they adjusted remarkably well to counter-insurgency, as well as dealing with conventional warfare and civilian irregulars. Whether building and defending an isolated CIDG camp, serving with larger MGFs, or operating on a small SOG team, Special Forces soldiers were highly motivated and determined to accomplish their missions at all costs.

When the Special Forces departed Vietnam, they accounted for 17 Medals of Honor, one Distinguished Service Medal, 60 Distinguished Service Crosses, 814 Silver Stars, 13,234 Bronze Stars, 235 Legions of Merit, 46 Distinguished Flying Crosses, 232 Soldier's Medals, 4,891 Air Medals, 6,908 Army Commendation Medals, and 2,658 Purple Hearts.

Mission after mission these warriors demonstrated their courage and tenacity to tackle the impossible and come out victorious. The men of the U.S. Army Special Forces, known to many as the "Green Berets," did their duty and departed from Southeast Asia with honor.

CHAPTER 4

Special Forces Beyond Vietnam

This modified version of the HUMMV for desert operations during Desert Shield/Storm was dubbed the DUMMV. Currently it's referred to as a Ground Mobility Vehicle (GMV). The ultimate 4x4 vehicle, it allowed SF soldiers to execute their mission at long range, or serve as a Mission Support Site (MSS), from which ODAs operate in their AO. This particular GMV is armed with a Mark 19, 40mm Grenade Machine gun, and is loaded with fuel cans, water, ammunition, and other mission-essential equipment. Attached to the rear of the vehicle is camouflage netting that may be deployed by the team to conceal its MSS.

I n the years following the Vietnam war the Special Forces saw a dramatic downsizing. The 1st, 3rd, 6th, and 8th Special Forces Groups were deactivated or consolidated into other groups. Conventional commanders were trying to distance themselves from the war in Southeast Asia and cast their attention anew on the verdant valleys of "cold-war" Europe. Beset by conventional commanders, Special Forces soldiers fought the Army mindset for mere survival. The Special Forces soldier had become an anachronism, and many people considered becoming a member to be a dead-end career path. During the early 1970s, the Army was placing more emphasis on the Rangers, and some of the SF missions were being incorporated into the two newly formed Ranger battalions. In January 1969 the JFK Institute for Special Warfare was renamed the U.S. Army JFK Institute for Military Assistance. (IMA)

In an attempt to maintain their capabilities, Special Forces commanders formulated the SPARTAN program. SPARTAN stood for Special Proficiency at Rugged Training and Nation Building. This program was created to demonstrate the many skills of the Special Forces soldier. It also proved that SF troops were not outdated merely because the United States was no longer engaged in active warfare.

The SPARTAN program sent soldiers from the 5th SFG(A) and 7th SFG(A) to various states throughout the United States, such as Florida, Arizona, and Montana, to work on American Indian reservations. Here the SF soldiers applied their talents on American soil, building roads, schools, medical facilities. They provided medical treatment to the poverty-stricken areas of Hoke and Anson counties in North Carolina. To this day, you can still find SF soldiers working among the American Indian population. Major Tom McCollum, SF-PAO, said, "going to these locations, our soldiers get the feel for real Third World conditions." As honorable as this program was, civic actions were not the primary purpose Special Forces had been intended to serve. Special Forces was created for unconventional warfare, and with the lessons learned in the Vietnam War, Special Forces missions would be broadened beyond Unconventional Warfare (UW) to include direct action in a guerrilla war. They would not have to wait too long for the opportunity to serve this role.

In November 1979 the U.S. Embassy in Teheran, Iran, was captured and its staff taken hostage. While alternate venues were discussed, President Jimmy Carter, after six months, authorized the military option, and Operation Eagle Claw commenced.

What began as an extraordinary attempt by the U.S. Special Operations Forces ended in tragedy in the darkness of an Iranian desert. It was April 1980 when Special Forces Operation Detachment - Delta, better known as "Delta Force," along with supporting Air Force and Marine aircraft and aircrews, met with disaster. Operation Eagle Claw had failed. It resulted in the loss of eight courageous troops and damaged the honor of the United States of America and the credibility of U.S. Special Operations.

Following the disaster at Desert One, a review committee known as the Holloway Commission convened to look into problems within U.S. Special Operations. At the conclusion of its review, the Commission made two major recommendations. First, the Department of Defense should establish a Counterterrorism Joint Task Force (CTJTF) as a field organization of the Joint Chiefs of Staff (JCS) with a permanently assigned staff and forces. The JCS would plan, train for, and conduct

Two members of Company C, 2nd Battalion, 7th SFG(A). Staff Sergeant John Anchex and Sergeant Rodney Allen (left to right) rappel down an icy mountain during Exercise Brim Frost, 1981. Rappelling skills are still used today when necessary to maneuver down a mountain slope, or down the side of a building as in SFAUC. *Defense Visual Information Center Photo*

operations to counter terrorist activities directed against the United States. The CTJTF would employ military forces in the counterterrorism (CT) role. These forces could range in size from small units of highly specialized personnel to larger integrated forces. Second, the JCS should consider the formation of a Special Operations Advisory Panel (SOAP). This panel would consist of high-ranking officers to be drawn from both active service and retired personnel. To be selected a soldier needed a background in special operations or service at a CinC or JCS level with proficient knowledge of special operations or defense policy.

With the election of President Ronald W. Reagan in 1980, the U.S. military would get a much-needed revitalization. The defense policy of the new administration, along with the emergence of anti-Leninist guerrillas in Nicaragua, Angola, Mozambique, and Afghanistan, compelled the United States to take a more dynamic role in combating communism. These situations also heightened the awareness of deficiencies in U.S. Special Operation Forces. A new focus came into being: Low Intensity Conflict, and the Army Special Forces in particular would benefit from this new attention.

On 1 June 1982, the Center for Military Assistance was redesignated the 1st Special Operations Command (Airborne) (SOCOM), and assigned to U.S. Army Forces Command (FORSCOM). FORSCOM was responsible for all activities of Special Operations Forces units. In June 1983 the IMA

During Exercise Team Spirit 1986 a member of the 1st Special Forces Groups (Airborne) assumes a prone firing position to provide security for his team as they secure the perimeter of the Pohang DZ (drop zone). Using his rucksack for cover, he aims his M-16 and watches for any OpFor (Opposition Force) soldiers. *Defense Visual Information Center Photo*

Kuwaiti soldiers from the 2nd Infantry Battalion, 15th Brigade, fire M-16 rifles on the firing line while being supervised by a U.S. Army Special Forces Sergeant First Class. Special Forces troops conducted live fire training with the Kuwaitis and instructed them on the use and care of M-16s and assorted small arms. They were part of the coalition forces who fought in Desert Storm. The working relationship and cultural experience the SF soldiers possess made the members of the SF ODAs (Operational Detachments-Alpha) "the glue that held the coalition together," per General Norman Schwarzkopf. *Defense Visual Information Center Photo*

was again named the U.S. Army John F. Kennedy Special Warfare Center. The qualification course for Special Forces was lengthened and toughened, so only the highest quality soldiers would make it to the SF A-teams. The A-teams were also slightly modified, with the executive officer changed from a lieutenant to a warrant officer. The A-teams remained the backbone of Special Forces. In October 1984 the Army established a separate career management field (CMF 18) for Special Forces soldiers. The warrant officer career

management field (CMF 180) was introduced shortly thereafter on 9 April 1987.

In October 1983 the United States mounted Operation Urgent Fury to rescue American medical students and suppress pro-communist insurgents on the island of Grenada. All the services, consisting fully of volunteer forces, wanted to show what they could do. Within two days of landing on the island on 15 October 1983, the island was secure. U.S. forces were victorious, but

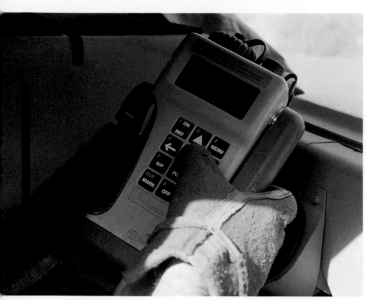

Using the Global Positioning System (GPS) unit, SF teams were able to determine their positions accurately as they performed SR, DA, and other missions across the wasteland of the Iraqi desert during the Gulf War.

various Third World countries. Special Forces played a pivotal role in El Salvador and Honduras, preventing a civil war in Nicaragua from spilling over the borders.

In May 1986, Congressmen William Cohen and Sam Nunn introduced a Senate bill to amend the 1986 Defense Authorizations Bill. The following month, Congressman Dan Daniel introduced a similar bill in the House of Representatives. This bill, signed into law in October 1986, in part directed the formation of a unified command responsible for special operations. In April 1987, the U.S. Special Operations Command (USSOCOM) was established at MacDill AFB, Florida, and Army General James J. Lindsay assumed command.

In June 1988 the SF training program was increased from approximately 21 weeks to a full six months. This increase included a three-week Special Forces Assessment and Selection. SFAS also changed assignment from a PCS (permanent change of station) to TDY (temporary duty); this created a more fluid flow of soldiers who volunteered for Special Forces. This new assessment tested the candidates both psychologically and physically. Consequently, any unsuitable candidate could be removed from the program before ever entering the SF training. Field time was lengthened from 63 to 100 days.

Another milestone for Special Forces came on 1 December 1989, when the U.S. Army Special Operations Command (Airborne) was created under USSOCOM. USASOC, commanded by a three-star general, would be responsible for all Army Special Operations Forces. This would include the Rangers, the 160th Special Operations Aviation Regiment and, of course, the Special Forces.

This new command would have its effectiveness battle-tested when President George Bush ordered the execution of Operation Just Cause in Panama in December 1989. Special Forces would

it appeared special operations units still needed better coordination.

In 1984 the 1st Special Forces Group (Airborne) was reactivated at Fort Lewis, Washington. On 9 April 1987 the chief of staff of the Army established the Special Forces as a separate office career branch of the service. Special Forces officers would now wear the Crossed Arrow insignia on their uniform collars and Jungle Green was designated as the Special Forces Branch color.

As the Reagan policy unfolded, Special Forces detachments were deployed to numerous countries around the world. Their main mission was Foreign Internal Defense (FID). Other missions included training allied armed forces to defend their countries, humanitarian assistance, medical care, and construction of roads and buildings in play a proactive part in the invasion, which lasted less than 24 hours.

Members of the 7th SFG(A), Company A, 3rd Battalion under the command of Major Kevin Higgins, secured and held the Pacora River Bridge, a vital crossing point. Special Forces soldiers, along with conventional troops, blocked a Panamanian Defense Forces (PDF) vehicle convoy from bringing reinforcements across the bridge. As they held the convoy, using LAW and AT-4 anti-tank weapons, an AC-130H Spectre gunship orbiting overhead employed precision fire, halting any further PDF movement.

In another part of the country, members of the 7th SFG(A) were tasked with the surgical mission of disabling a television repeater facility at Cero Azul. As Operation Just Cause began on 19 December 1989, two MH-60 helicopters lifted off for their target. Aboard these two aircraft was an 18-man element of Special Forces soldiers, augmented with members of the 1109th Signal Battalion.

Once on site, they fast-roped to the ground and, using explosives, neutralized the target. While the signalmen went to work on the electronics equipment, the SF soldiers swept the building, making sure it was secure, and conducted patrols in the local area. With the mission complete without taking any enemy fire, they extracted by MH-60 Blackhawks.

A year later, U.S. Army Special Forces Command (USASFC), which assumed command of all SF units, was established as a Major Subordinate Command, or MSC. A second MSC, USACAPOC (U.S. Army Civil Affairs and Psychological Operations Command), would be included under USASOC. USACAPOC included all PsyWar and civil affairs units. In June 1990 USASOC also took over command of the JFK Institute and School from TRADOC (Training and Doctrine Command). All of the capabilities and components of the Army Special Operations Forces were now under U.S. Army Special Operations Command (Airborne), or USASOC.

In the beginning of 1991, USASOC and the Special Forces would be called to war again in the vast desert wasteland of Southwest Asia. Operation Desert Shield was launched after Iraq invaded the neighboring country of Kuwait. National Command Authority (NCA) immediately deployed members of the 3rd, 5th, and 10th Special Forces Groups (Airborne), along with Civil Affairs and Psychological Operations units, to the Persian Gulf region. Special Operations Command Central, or SOCCENT, was responsible for the area abutting the Iraqi border, some 60,000 square miles of desert. Unlike their Panamanian mission, when U.S. Special Operations Forces went to war this time, they operated with a new set of parameters: Is this an appropriate SOF mission? Does it support the CinC's campaign plan? Is it operationally feasible? Are the required resources available to execute? Does the expected outcome justify the risk?

The primary mission of the Special Forces soldiers as Operation Desert Shield began was to work with their FID skills in the formation of a defensive posture among the newly formed Coalition Forces. The 5th Special Forces Group's mission of Coalition Assistance came to the forefront at this time. Due to its constant deployment into the theater and working relationship with the local military, the 5th SFG(A) was familiar with the areas, languages, and cultures of these soldiers. They also knew the abilities of these forces and how they operated in this region. This mission also included members of 10th Special Forces Group, who interacted with coalition members from Europe, e.g., British, French, Czech, and so on. Because of the SF soldiers' expertise, they worked with almost every level of Coalition Forces, 109 battalions in total. They were instrumental in establishing working relations with the Saudi, Egyptian, and Syrian military.

Under camouflage netting, the GMVs are well hidden in the MSS. Captain Steve Warman of ODA581 receives a communication over the SatCom radio. While the team leader sends in a situation report, or SitRep, Commo Sergeant Christopher Spence provides security, keeping a watchful eye on the terrain.

During Operation Desert Storm, Special Forces ODAs (Operational Detachments-Alpha) would conduct deep reconnaissance in Saudi Arabia, Iraq, and Kuwait. These recon missions not only provided up-to-the-minute intel on the Iraqi forces, but included analyzing soil conditions to ascertain whether it would support the heavy weight of armored vehicles. In addition to the special reconnaissance (SR) mission, the ODAs would perform direct action (DA) missions, e.g., sabotaging lines of communication, raids, ambushes, and destroying command and control targets. They also assisted in Combat Search and Rescue (CSAR) missions and supported the Kuwaiti resistance.

As the air war began, SF teams were tasked with behind-the-lines intelligence-gathering missions. One such SR mission was carried out by ODA-525 of the 5th SFG(A), under the command of CWO2 John "Bulldog" Balwanz. Chief Balwanz relates that 5th SFG-Desert Shield basically started with coalition work, beginning with border recon on Saudi and Kuwaiti borders. The group was using DUMMVs—HUMMVs modified for desert operations. They were on the border between Saudi and Kuwait; they were the eyes of the command. ODA-525 was located at the King Fahad airport, along with the 1st Battalion of the 5th SFGF and SOCCENT. This underground command center was known as the "Bat Cave."

Balwanz had his team running training missions—cross country movement, long range movements, including areas in the Northwest portion of Saudi, near the Jordan border. They also began rehearsing such things as building hide sites. There was no SOP for desert hide sites, so in the tradition of good SF soldiers the team scrounged and scavenged material. King Fahad airport was under construction at this time, so procurement was not a problem. Soon the SF troopers had assorted lengths of metal conduit on hand to fabricate their hide site. The basic hide site consisted of a hole, approximately nine feet square and five feet deep dug into the desert. Up from the hole came the center stand, which was an umbrella-like device with arms that stretched over the hole. The whole assembly was then covered with plastic, then burlap, then topped off with sand, making the hide site blend into the terrain. This whole assembly would then be broken down and carried in the soldiers' rucksacks. An average hide site kit could weigh more than 100 pounds.

Finally, the word came down that ODA-525 had its SR mission. Chief Balwanz and his team were moved from King Fahad airport to King Khalid Military City (KKMC), which was the staging area for the 5th Special Forces group. During Isolation, all details of the mission were gone over, and the list of needed equipment was decided upon by the team. When the team inserted into Iraq, each man's rucksack, including the hide site kit, weighed over 175 pounds. Chief Balwanz relates that "Along with the kit, there was 5 gallons of water per man, ammunition, food, shovels, extra batteries, redundant radio systems. We had two SatCom systems, a system to talk with the aircraft, and even a PRC-104 radio for emergencies." In addition to all this equipment, four of the team members carried M-16A2 rifles, two carried M-16s outfitted with M-203 grenade launchers, the last two carried the HK MP5 SD3 suppressed 9mm submachine guns; all members of the team also carried the M-9, 9mm Beretta as a sidearm.

On the morning of 23 February 1991, Chief Balwanz and the men of ODA-525 loaded onto two MH-60 Blackhawks of the 160th Special Operations Aviation Regiment (Airborne)—the "Night Stalkers." This would be the first time in the history of the Army that a warrant officer would lead a team into combat. The team was prepared to stay on the ground for four days. At the end of four days, they would be extracted, or if the ground war had begun by this time, they would link up with the ground force as the corps passed through their position. (They did not know when they loaded the helicopters that the ground war was scheduled to begin the next morning.) Chief Balwanz relates a conversation with Chief Warrant Officer 3 Kenny Collier. CWO3 Collier was a former SF soldier, now a helicopter pilot with the 160th SOAR. He would be piloting one of the MH-60s that would be inserting ODA-525. "Kenny," Chief Balwanz said, "I know you'll get me in . . . [my] concern is you coming back for me." With a smile on his face

Chief Collier assured his friend and fellow warrior, "I tell you, dog . . . you call, we'll haul!"

"Our mission called for us to go about 150 miles into Iraq," says Balwanz. "We wanted to put eyes on a major highway, Highway 7. It ran from Baghdad to Nasiriyah, then cut over to Basara." This put them in the right spot to provide "hard" intel to the corps commander once the ground war began. Were the Iraqis sending in reinforcements, or were they withdrawing their troops? They would locate their hide site in the area of the Euphrates River. Since there would be some vegetation, the SF soldiers opted to wear standard issue woodland BDUs (battle dress uniforms), rather than the desert "chocolate chip" or three-color desert camouflage patterns.

They flew from KKMC to Rahfa, just inside the Iraqi boarder, to refuel the Blawkhawks. Fuel would be a critical factor in inserting the SR team. Mission planners had determined that infil and exfil would be done with only 10 minutes of fuel to spare. This also meant that if ODA-525 hit a hot LZ, they had less than 10 minutes to get the helicopters back out. Timing was also critical because the team needed to be on the ground a certain number of hours to build their hide sites before the sun came up. The plan called for a departure at 2000 hours, refuel at 2200, and getting on site with six hours before first light.

As the two helicopters flew into the Iraqi night, the pilots got word that the mission had been aborted, and they returned toward Rahfa. As they landed in Rahfa, they were told that it was on again. While there is a lot of speculation as to why this happened, no one ever gave clear reason. With the mission back on, the MH-60 needed to refuel. This ate up valuable darkness time and placed the team behind schedule for the insertion.

Fuel tanks now topped off, and the insertion window getting smaller, the MH-60s took off. The pilots were flying on NVGs (night vision goggles) approximately 20 feet above the desert at

During Operation Uphold Democracy, Brigadier General Meade studies maps and aerial photos with a group of Special Forces soldiers. The general is being briefed by the SF members after a grenade attack in Port au Prince, Haiti, that killed five people and wounded another 25. *Defense Visual Information Center Photo*

more than 120 knots. It was hazardous moving so low and fast, and all of a sudden the Blackhawk jerked up. Chief Balwanz, wearing a head set, inquired what had happened. Chief Collier calmly responded, "We just hit a sand dune, probably tore off the rear landing gear."

Well hell, thought Bulldog, if Kenny isn't worried, then I'm not going to worry about it, either.

Shortly thereafter, a flock of ducks flew up from a lake or pond and one got sucked into one of the engines, shutting it down. This still did not deter the pilots of the 160th.

As they got close to their target site, they performed a couple of false insertions. They would intentionally get picked up on enemy radar, then sit down on the ground 10–15 seconds, then move to another site. As they neared their predetermined site, another snag arose. Due to the recall, they had lost global position system (GPS) satellite coverage, so the pilots went to alternate navigational systems that are not as accurate.

As the two Blackhawks touched down, the eight-man SF team—four men from each helicopter—jumped to the ground and assumed a defensive position on the desert surface. They had been told there would be no dogs, but moments after landing the air filled with barking. They removed their PVS7 NVGs and let their eyes acclimate to the night and their surroundings. By now the GPS was back online, and the team found out it was about a mile from its planned insertion spot. The men broke out the map and a compass, hoisted their 175-pound packs, and headed to the spot they had selected for their hide sites.

After moving about 3/4 mile, they stopped to cache the PRC-104, an FM radio capable of Morse code. If everything went south, they could get to the radio and E&E out of the area. Each member of the team had the GPS location of the site; there was also a small palm tree at the position so it would be easy for them to locate.

The team members moved on, finally reaching the canal where they planned to establish their hide sites. When they rehearsed digging hide sites in Saudi, the soil was soft loam, but here the ground was rock hard. There was no way the team would be able to replicate the Saudi-style hide site in the allotted time before daylight. They decided to dig into the side of the canal where the earth was softer. One team set up a hasty hide site in the canal, while the other dropped back a little where the ground was looser. From the highway either site would be invisible.

The team split, digging two separate hide sites 150 meters apart and approximately 300–400 meters from the highways. One group would watch the northbound traffic, the other the southbound. They needed to be close to the road so they could identify "signature items," pieces of equipment that are specific to a particular division or type of unit. As Chief Balwanz explained, "If you could ID the equipment, then you could ID the unit." Close proximity also allowed them to identify whether a tank was a Soviet T-72 or a T-55.

As the sun rose, the men in the hide site heard the sound of children playing. The children came closer to the site and looked inside, seeing team member SSgt. James Weatherford. Startled, the children ran away. Immediately, the team medic, Sgt. Daniel Kostrzebski, and weapons specialist, SFC Robert Degroff, were out the rear of the hide site with their weapons sighted on the fleeing children. They asked Chief Balwanz what they should do. Knowing full well that if the children made it back to their homes, the team would be compromised, he told his men not to shoot. The team gathered in the canal and via the SatCom contacted XVIII Airborne Corps, informing them they had been compromised and requesting immediate exfiltration.

The hide sites being compromised, Chief Balwanz instructed his team sergeants to stay in the canal and once it became dark, they would move to a new location and continue their mission. All was going well, until just after noon. At this time, CWO2 Balwanz was leaning on the parapet of the canal, observing the highway with his binoculars, when another group of children discovered them. A sheepherder also saw them and began heading quickly back to the village. The team again contacted base, requesting an exfil and possibly close air support (CAS). They were told that emergency exfiltration would be mobilized and that CAS was 20 minutes out.

A group of Bedouins came out looking for the team, and shortly afterward, four or five trucks, a Toyota Land Cruiser, and a bus stopped on the highway. An estimated 150 Iraqi soldiers armed with weapons poured from the vehicles and began to move toward the ODA-525's canal site. Sensing an imminent firefight, Chief Balwanz put into effect their emergency destruct plan: All the team's classified crypto gear, radios, and burst equipment were stuffed into one of the rucksacks and rigged with a block of C4 explosive that was then set with a one minute timer. The team piled the rest of their rucksacks on top of it. Carrying only their weapons, load-bearing equipment (LBE), with ammunition and water, and one LST-5 SatCom radio, the SF soldiers ran down the canal. The Iraqis, plus the Bedouins, began maneuvering around the eight-man SF team. As the team tried to put some distance between themselves and the enemy, they heard the C4 explode and the screams of Iraqi soldiers. This meant that the Iraqis were about a minute behind them.

Their pursuers began firing and were trying to outflank them. Chief Balwanz ordered his two M-203 gunners (SFCs Degroff and Hovermale) to start laying down fire. The team was now located in an "elbow' of the canal, with nowhere else to run. Fortunately, the troops closing in on the Americans were not aware they had stumbled on an SF team; perhaps they thought it was just a downed aircrew. Secondly, these were not Republican Guards, they were more militia-type soldiers. They tended to bunch up and walk upright, firing on the SF soldiers. When the 40mm HE rounds went off, these bunches became history. In the first minute of the firefight Chief Balwanz and his men took out almost 40 of the enemy. Another advantage for ODA-525 was that five of its eight men were school-trained snipers. They did not have any sniper rifles, but at 300 to 500 meters, their training made a real difference in the fight. Precise shooting also allowed the team to conserve its ammunition.

Finally, over the LST-5 they could hear the Forward Air Controller calling for the team. Unfortunately, in their haste to destroy the radio gear, the VHF whip antennae for the LST-5 had been left behind. Although the team could hear the aircraft, they could not communicate with them. As a last resort, SFC Degroff pulled his PRC-90 survival radio out and tried to make contact with any coalition aircraft. After a number of attempts, he got a response from an AWACS, which then passed the team's frequency on to the U.S. Air Force F-16s there to provide CAS.

While the Falcon pilots had yet to establish the actual location of the team, their mere presence caused many of the Iraqis to run away from the beleaguered SF team. At last the flight detected the team's position. The first request from the team was to take care of the vehicle and the people on the highway. The F-16s made their run dropping cluster bomb units (CBU). One minute there were vehicles, the next there was nothing but burning scrap metal. Now the attention of the CAS was directed at those enemy soldiers closing in on the team. Flying at 20,000 feet, the F-16 pilots were dropping CBU approximately 200 meters, or "danger close" to the SF soldiers. A total of 16 sorties were flown in support of ODA-525 that day.

As daylight faded, the team fought back down the canal and the fight died down. The helicopters were now inbound. The team returned to the cached PRC-90 radio, which was equipped with a beacon. They turned the unit to beacon mode and after a couple of minutes, two MH-60s descended almost right on top of the team. In less than ten seconds the team was on board. The helicopters lifted into the night sky and headed back to KKMC. Chief Balwanz was awarded the Silver Star, and the balance of the team was awarded the Bronze Star with V-device. The Blackhawk pilots received the Distinguished Flying Cross, and their crew members were awarded Air Medals.

Special Forces ODAs continued to perform similar missions even deeper as Operation Desert Storm began the ground phase of the war. SF teams shadowed the Iraqi Republican Guard, and every move they made was immediately reported to General Schwarzkopf's command center. This gave the CinC the vital, up-to-the minute information he required to mount the offensive that would decimate the Iraqi forces. In one of his briefings, General Schwarzkopf acknowledged that the Special Forces teams "let us know what was going on out there, and they were the eyes out there."

In summation, the ODAs of the U.S. Army Special Forces put their principles of coalition warfare into reality, combining the synergy of three allied corps into a united force that liberated Kuwait. General Schwarzkopf would say of the Special Forces, "They were the glue that held the coalition together."

After the Gulf War, in April 1991, members of the 1st Battalion, 10th Special Forces Groups (Airborne), were deployed to southeast Turkey and northern Iraq to participate in Operation Provide Comfort. Here the SF soldiers were involved in humanitarian operations with more than a half-million Kurdish refugees. As the month wore on, the 2nd and finally the 3rd Battalion would join in the operation, resulting in the deployment of the entire 10th group. The SF teams were instrumental in saving these refugees, as they provided direction, overall ground relief, and security for the operational activities.

As the missions wound down in the Persian Gulf region, Special Forces teams found themselves occupied with training schedules and new missions to carry out, as the latest operations unveiled themselves. Members of the 2nd Battalion, 5th SFG(A), were involved in Operation Restore Hope and Provide Comfort on the continent of Africa. They were placed under the command of the Joint Special Operations Forces, a component command of the Unified Task Force. When the detachment deployed to Somalia, the men established an Advance Operations Base (AOB) and began their initial mission of border surveillance along the Ethiopian boarder. Their mission was to locate and identify members of Somalian factions and bandits using Ethiopia as sanctuary while they carried out raids into Somalia.

In January of 1993, the SF forward operating base, or FOB, deployed to Mogadishu and assumed command and control of Joint Special

The United States leads de-mining operations around the world. Members of the SF are instrumental in teaching host nations' troops the proper methods of safely dealing with the plethora of mines scattered across the battlefields. Here a soldier from the 10th SFG(A) buries an inert land mine, which will be used to teach students the finer points of probing. *Defense Visual Information Center Photo*

Operation – Somalia (JSOFOR). JSOFOR organized and conducted Special Operations in Somalia in support of the UNITAF humanitarian relief efforts.

JSOFOR originated with a small force of one Operational Detachment B, or ODB, five ODA operating out of Belet Uen, and one ODA in Bardera. These forces supported operations under the UNITAF area of responsibility ranging from the Indian Ocean in the South to the Ethiopian boarder in the North. This area was subsequently divided into nine sections referred to as Humanitarian Relief Sectors (HRS); SF would be employed in four of the nine sectors.

The SF ODA units proved themselves a valuable asset to the task force. On one occasion SF soldiers made contact with an Ethiopian boarder post after 10 days of diplomatic efforts had failed. Making this connection with the post created a relationship that would provide valuable intelligence regarding the movement of Somali factions along the border.

While Operation Restore Hope did have some success in Somalia, any benefits these SF soldiers contributed in carrying out their missions faded into the background. Somalia will be remembered by the firefight in October 1993 involving Task Force Ranger, resulting in 18 U.S. soldiers killed and more than 30 wounded; enemy losses were estimated at more than 1,000.

On the other side of the globe, SF soldiers were participating in Operation Uphold Democracy on the island of Haiti. Members of the 3rd SFG(A) were sent to Haiti to establish an FOB, while the bulk of conventional troops of the 10th Mountain Division and later the 25th Infantry secured the city in Port au Prince. SF ODAs would deploy to the FOB and then fan out into the countryside in order to stabilize the remainder of the island.

During Haitian operations, a Special Forces captain and his men were making their way through a village. Three women approached him pleading for their assistance. The women told the SF captain that the local "witch" had placed a curse on their children and they wanted the American officers to help them. The so-called witch in question just sat there glaring at the soldiers. This was definitely something out of the ordinary for these men.

The captain slung his M-4 carbine over his shoulder and pondered the situation. Had the women told him there were rebels in the hills, he could call in helicopters; had he been informed that armored cars were attacking civilians, he had Spectre gunships at hand; but a "witch" was well beyond the scope of normal mission parameters.

As he deliberated over the predicament, the captain stuck his hand in the pocket of his BDU. There he found a small chemical light stick. Secretly he snapped the stick, allowing the chemicals to mix, thus creating a soft glow. Shielding the light from view, he pulled the light stick out of his pocket and held it behind his thumb. With the other hand he removed his combat knife from its sheath. In a deliberate and careful move he cut what appeared to be the tip of his thumb, in reality the top of the chemlight. As the light mixture started to ooze out, the SF captain gently rubbed a small mark on the forehead of each of the children. All eyes, now wide with awe, were on the captain. He told the women this would protect their children from any curses or spells. Then he told the "witch" that she was to leave these mothers and children alone, or he would return. This is exactly what Special Forces soldiers are trained to do, to think "outside the box."

Operational Tempo, or OpTempo, as it is called, remained continually high for members of the Special Forces, as the United States committed more than 20,000 American soldiers to the country of Bosnia. In December 1995, a joint NATO (North Atlantic Treaty Organization) force would deploy to this war-torn country to partake in Operation Joint Endeavor as the military elements of the Dayton Peace Accords. The first of the U.S. units to enter Bosnia-Herzegovina would come from the 10th SFG(A). Further operations in this region would find the SF soldiers of the 3rd & 10th groups involved in Operations Joint Guard and Joint Forge.

Additionally, the 10th SFG(A) would be active in Operation Joint Guardian in Kosovo. As members of the Kosovo Forces (KFOR), SF teams

Staff Sergeant Gary Koenitzer of ODA-126, 1st Special Force Group (Airborne), takes a break with his students in southern Thailand. These Thai troops are being instructed in patrolling, small unit, and unconventional warfare tactics. *Courtesy MSgt. Gary Koenitzer*

employed their unique skills and cultural abilities in this region. During the early stages of American involvement, NATO planes began an air campaign over the skies of Kosovo in spring of 1999. When a U.S. Air Force F-117 Nighthawk was downed, members of the 10th SFG(A) who were on alert for possible CSAR (Combat Search And Rescue) missions were loaded onto waiting helicopters within 10 minutes of getting the information.

Members of the 3rd, 10th SFG(A), and selected SF National Guard units participated in all major operations in the Balkans. Special Forces teams were instrumental in the peacekeeping efforts in this region, and provided SF liaison control elements to the NATO allies and coalition partners. As of this writing, ODAs from the 10th SFG(A) are still active in Bosnia and Kosovo. The 5th SFG(A) has teams active in Kuwait. SF soldiers of the 3rd SFG(A) are conducting missions throughout the continent of Africa as part of the African Crisis Response Initiative (ACRI). ODAs from the 7th SFG(A) are performing FID and Counter-Drug (CD) training for national police and military forces in the jungles of Colombia, and members of the 1st SFG(A) carry out their missions in the Asia-Pacific region. Whether they are part of a larger operation or a single A-Detachment—perhaps the only U.S. military presence in a country—the sun never sets on the U.S. Army Special Forces.

Special Forces Organization and Missions

Today's Special Forces is founded on a rich heritage and warrior lineage. The modern SF soldiers draw their combat skills from the proud tradition of their special warfare predecessors—the "Swamp Fox," the Office of Strategic Service (OSS) Jedburg teams, 1st Special Service Forces, and others. Members of the U.S. Army Special Forces still espouse the ensign held up by President John F. Kennedy. Kennedy gave the men of the Special Forces more than the green beret; he gave them a mission: to uphold democracy at all costs. Over the past five decades this standard has been carried into various conflicts, and the men of the Special Forces have paid the price. At the height of the Vietnam War there were more than a dozen Special Forces Groups, including active, Army Reserve, and National Guard units.

Today, under the command of Brigadier General Frank J. Toney Jr., the U.S. Army Special Forces Command (Airborne), USASFC(A), commands seven major subordinate units (or groups), each commanded by a colonel. The mission statement of the SF Command is "To organize, equip, train, validate and prepare forces for deployment to conduct worldwide special operations, across the range of military operations, in support of regional combatant commanders, American ambassadors and other agencies as directed."

Special Forces units are oriented to specific areas around the world. By concentrating on specific regions, the SF soldiers gain experience in the regional culture and languages of their assigned countries. This also gives them the opportunity to form a bond with the foreign mil-

itary forces and a working relationship with the indigenous population. There are five active SF groups: the 1st SFG(A), 3rd SFG(A), 5th SFG(A), 7th SFG(A), and 10th SFG(A). In addition to these active units, there are two National Guard SF groups, the 19th SFG(A) and 20th SFG(A). In addition to the Special Forces Groups, USASFC(A)

The modern SF soldiers draw their combat skills from the proud tradition of their special warfare predecessors. As with the OSS Jedburgh teams of World War II, airborne insertion is a hallmark trait of the Special Forces soldier. This SF team prepares for an over-the-water insertion via parachute. They wait in the cavernous fuselage of the C-130 for the signal to jump. The red lights allow their eyes to adjust to the darkness.

The SF soldiers may find themselves operating in a variety of environments, from the tropical rain forest of South America to the desert sands of the Middle East; from the jungles of Africa to the snow-covered mountainsides of Europe and the Balkans. Natural surroundings may pose as much danger as any foe. Fortunately, SF soldiers are proficient at dealing with both circumstances.

Beret Flashes of the U.S. Army Special Operations (Left to Right) Top Row: U.S. Army Special Operations Command (Airborne), U.S. Army Special Forces Command (Airborne), U.S. Army John F. Kennedy Special Warfare Center & School (Airborne), and U.S. Army Special Warfare Training Group (Airborne). Middle Row (Active): 1st Special Forces Group (Airborne), 3rd Special Forces Group (Airborne), 5th Special Forces Group (Airborne), 7th Special Forces Group (Airborne), and 10th Special Forces Group (Airborne). Bottom Row (National Guard): 20th Special Forces Group (Airborne) and 10th Special Forces Group (Airborne).

also has two active duty and two reserve chemical recon detachments (not SF personnel) and a 13-man SF detachment, assigned to 1st SFG(A) to support theater war-planning requirements on the Korean peninsula, known as Detachment K or Det-K.

The 1st Special Forces Group (Airborne) has its headquarters in Ft. Lewis, Washington. Their motto is "Warriors First—First in Asia." Under the authority of PACOM (Pacific command) this group has a pre-deployed battalion or ODB stationed on the island of Okinawa. Additionally,

the 1st SFG(A) provides soldiers for Detachment K in Korea. Their area of responsibility (AOR) is the Pacific rim and Asia, which includes all the islands up through India, Manchuria, and China. Also, due to its size, part of Russia also falls under their AOR. The 1st Group maintains a high state of preparedness to carry out special operations in support of USCINCPAC (U.S. Commander In Chief Pacific) in a major theater war.

The 3rd SFG(A) is based at Ft. Bragg, North Carolina, and is assigned to EUCOM (European Command), concentrating mainly on the continent of Africa, excluding the Horn of Africa. Third Group also has one battalion that is on line to support CENTCOM (Central Command), which is

The Special Forces soldier is often the eyes and the ears of a theater commander. Members of the SF teams hold a minimum grade of E-5 sergeant. Each soldier is a mature, physically rugged, morally straight, thoroughly lethal, and highly skilled individual who brings a new level of professionalism to an already elite military unit.

The team leader of the SF ODA (Operational Detachment-Alpha) is a captain. He will spend two years as a detachment commander before he moves on to other assignments within the Special Operations Forces (SOF) community. Occasionally, a team leader will get an additional rotation with the teams; however, this is the exception rather than the rule. Unique in their operations from a conventional infantry commander, the SF captain team leaders take on missions and encounter obstacles that not only require unconventional military measures, but also require unorthodox thinking.

responsible for the Middle East. One of the major missions involving the 3rd SFG(A) is the African Crisis Response Initiative, or ACRI. This is a prime example of an SF collateral mission, that of security assistance. ACRI is a U.S. Department of State-supported program intended to enhance the security and peace in selected countries on the continent of Africa. SF ODAs (Operational Detachments-Alpha) will train soldiers from these countries into highly effective and rapid-deployable peacekeeping units. With this training, the local forces can be used as peacekeeping forces, thus limiting or perhaps even eliminating the need for large U.S. involvement.

Next is 5th SFG(A), located in Ft. Campbell, Kentucky. It is the lead Group under CENTCOM. Their AOR is from the Horn of Africa up through the Central Asia Republics of Kazakhstan, Turkmenistan, and Tajikistan. While it does not have

a forward deployed battalion, like the 1st Group, the 5th SFG(A) does regularly rotate an ODA through the Middle East, maintaining a constant presence in Kuwait. The exploits of the 5th Group are legendary. From the jungles of Vietnam to the desert wastelands in Iraq, the men of 5th SFG(A) have set a benchmark in Special Forces operations.

If you travel north on Ft. Bragg's Yadin Road and hang a right at 77th SFG Way, you'll locate the HQ for the 7th SFG(A). Its motto is "Lo Que Sera, Cuando Sera, Donde Sera" (Anything, Anytime, Anyplace). They operate the SOUTHCOM (South Command) AOR in Central and South America and the Caribbean. One company of the 7th SFG(A) is forward based in Puerto Rico, at Roosevelt Roads Naval Air Station, or "Roosey Roads," as it is called. Additionally, members of the 7th have been selected to participate in the Army WarFighter Experiment exercises, to test new SF doctrine, organization, and equipment.

Finally, under EUCOM, is the 10th Special Forces Group (Airborne) based out of Ft. Carson, Colorado. It also has a forward deployed battalion in Panzer Kaserne, Boeblingen, Germany. This AOR for the 10th Group comprises Europe and countries of the former Soviet Union, including Russia (except for the part handled by 1st SFG(A)). The 10th Group holds the honor of being the original SF Group. If that seems confusing, it was meant to be. The Special Forces were created in the early 1950s to prepare a specialized force in the event of a World War III. They were to conduct guerrilla operations behind enemy lines, should the Soviets invade Europe. The U.S. Army only had one Special Forces unit at this time, but it did not want the Soviets to realize this—hence, this Special Forces Group was designated the 10th. The 10th SFG(A) was stationed in Bad Tolz, Germany, during the Cold War, and subsequently relocated to the Stuttgart area in July 1991. While the 10th Group encompasses all of the SF doctrinal missions, its ODAs hone their skills in unconventional warfare (UW), and they remain the premier mountain and winter troops among the U.S. Army Special Forces.

In November 1990, the Reserve SF Groups were deactivated, leaving only the National Guard Groups. The 19th SFG(A), a National Guard outfit with headquarters in Salt Lake City, Utah, has units spread throughout the western United States. The 19th group is a "jack of all trades." It operates in the Pacific, it has the ability to operate one battalion in Central Command, and it performs duties around Europe. The other Guard

If the SF team is the eyes and the ears of the CinC, then the eyes and ears of the SF ODA are the Operations and Intelligence Sergeants. These senior non-commissioned officers (NCOs) "run" the teams. They are the quintessential SF soldier. They thrive on ambiguity and uncertainty, thinking the unconventional and daring the uncommon. They see obstacles as something to be overcome, surroundings as environments to be adapted to, and tasks as opportunities for improvisation. A team sergeant will immerse himself in the art, science, and history of war.

outfit is the 20th SFG(A) with headquarters in Birmingham, Alabama, and units throughout the eastern United States. The 20th operates mostly in the Caribbean and Central and South America.

When you look around the world, you do not see large armored or infantry divisions in all places, yet Special Forces has a constant presence. So valuable are the SF groups that the CinC of EUCOM recently requested two additional SF Groups for his AOR.

The purpose of the SF Group is to establish, support, and operate a Special Forces Operational

The SF Weapons sergeants are responsible for the employment of weapons using conventional and UW tactics and techniques. They will serve as the detachment armorer. Here can be seen both light arms, M4A1 carbine, and heavier weapons, the AT-4 anti-tank weapon. The weapons sergeant will be an expert on both U.S. and foreign weapons systems and the best way to employ them.

staff personnel to operate an SFOB, and providing advice, coordination, and staff assistance on the employment of SF assets to a joint Special Operations Command (SOC), Joint Special Operations Task Force (JSOTF), or other major headquarters. The Support Company will provide military intelligence, signal support, and general aviation support. Each of these Battalions in turn comprises a Headquarters and three SF Companies.

The SF Battalion operates like the Group on a smaller scale. It conducts and supports any special operation in any operational environment, whether in peace, conflict, or war. The SF Company, also referred to as SFODB (Special Forces Operational Detachment-B or B-Team), consists of five ODAs or A-teams. SFODB has the capability to plan and carry out SF missions; train and prepare ODA for deployment; infiltrate and exfiltrate by air, land, or sea; conduct operations in remote areas and hostile environments for extended periods; and organize, equip, and train indigenous troops up to a regimental size. When you total all the personnel, you end up with approximately 1,200 people per SF Group, or 10,000 worldwide.

Each SF battalion will have one HALO (High Altitude Low Opening) team, schooled in Military Free Fall, MFF; one SCUBA (Self-Contained Underwater Breathing Apparatus) team, trained as Combat Swimmers; and one CT or Counterterrorist team. The balance of the teams are referred to as ruck teams, and they use the "low impact" method of insertion—by foot.

The A-team

The ODA remains the essence of the U.S. Army Special Forces. Here is where the "rucksack meets the ground," where missions are carried out. No matter how you got to that point, HALO, SCUBA, Ground Mobility Vehicle (GMV), Zodiac, or Helicopter, here is where the planning is put into action. The ODA is specifically designed

Base, SFOB, and Forward Operational Base, FOB, to provide special operation command and control units to conventional headquarters. The SF Group is responsible for training and preparing the SF ODA for deployment, and directing, supporting, and sustaining those ODA once deployed. Under each of these Groups, you'll find a Headquarters/Headquarters Company (HHC), a Support unit, and three SF Battalions.

The HHC plans, coordinates, and directs SF operations, either separately or as part of a larger force. This includes training and preparing SF teams for deployment, providing command and

Without a doubt the **green beret** headgear sets the U.S. Army Special Forces soldier apart from other troopers. It has become part of American folk history like the coonskin hat and cowboy hat. The hat was first sported by the members of the 10th SFG(A) in the Bavarian mountain ranges. The men would order the berets from a woolen company in Canada at their own expense, usually $7 to $8, in 1955. According to Mr. Joe Lupyak SF-CSM-ret., "The berets were only worn in the field, during exercises. [The Army] would not allow the wearing of the berets in garrison."

The green beret was originally designated in 1953 by Special Forces Major Herbert Brucker, a veteran of the OSS. Later that year, 1st Lt. Roger Pezelle adopted the beret as the unofficial headgear for his A-team, Operational Detachment FA32. Soon it spread throughout all of the Special Forces troops—much to the dismay of the U.S. Army and conventional commanders.

In 1961, President John F. Kennedy planned to visit Fort Bragg. He sent word to Brigadier General William P. Yarborough, the commander of the Special Warfare Center, that all Special Forces soldiers were to wear the green berets for this visit. President Kennedy felt that since they had a special mission, Special Forces should have something to set them apart from the rest of the conventional troops. Coincidentally, even before the presidential request came, the Department of the Army had reversed its objections to the headgear and sent a message to the center authorizing the green beret as part of the Special Forces uniform.

When President Kennedy arrived at Fort Bragg on 12 October 1961, Brigadier General William P. Yarborough wore his beret to greet the commander-in-chief. The president said, "Those are nice. How do you like the green beret?" Yarborough responded, "They're fine, sir. We've wanted them a long time."

President Kennedy sent a message to General Yarborough, stating, "My congratulations to you personally for your part in the presentation today . . . The challenge of this old but new form of operations is a real one and I know that you and the members of your command will carry on for us and the free world in a manner which is both worthy and inspiring. I am sure that the green beret will be a mark of distinction in the trying times ahead."

On 11 April 1962, in a White House memorandum for the United States Army, President Kennedy showed his continued support for the Special Forces, calling the green beret, "a symbol of excellence, a badge of courage, a mark of distinction in the fight for freedom."

Over the years, the custom of the green beret changed in Special Forces. When the first Special Forces wore the berets, they would only wear them in the field and never in garrison. Today, 50 years later, the green berets are worn only in garrison and rarely, if ever, are they worn in the field or on operations. There are a few exceptions to this rule. When meeting foreign military for the first time, the SF captain or sergeant may wear his green beret to receive instant credibility. Also, an NCOIC, or Non-Commissioned Officer In Charge, who is training local troops might wear the beret for immediate recognition by the indigenous troops.

Talk to some SF soldiers and they will tell you it is just a headgear, while others will explain that the green beret is the quickest way of identifying a member of the U.S. Army Special Forces, when starting to discuss Special Operation Forces. Either way, when an SF soldier places that green beret on his head, he walks a little straighter, and stands a little taller.

The **arrowhead** patch is worn by members of the Special Forces around the world. Drawing from the heritage of American Indians, the arrowhead depicts the field craft, stealth, and tactics of these tenacious warriors. The upturned dagger is symbolic of the nature of Special Forces unconventional warfare missions. The three lightning bolts represent the three methods of infiltration—land, sea, and air. Lightning is also characteristic of

SF Insignias

intense speed and strength. The color gold exemplifies fortitude and inspiration, and the teal blue background represents the Special Forces' encompassing of all branch assignments.

The distinctive **Special Forces crest** is black and silver, emblazoned with the Special Forces motto: De Oppresso Liber. This Latin phrase translates into To Free the Oppressed. A fighting knife is upturned and placed over two crossed arrows. The arrow symbolizes the Special Forces' role in unconventional warfare, and the knife reflects the attributes of a Special Forces soldier, straight and true. Both arrow and knife were silent weapons employed by the American Indians, thus providing a further link to the warrior spirit of this great nation.

In April of 1987 a new and separate branch of the Army was created for Special Forces officers. Prior to this time, officers assigned to Special Forces would wear the symbol for their branch of service on their collars, e.g. infantry, engineers, etc. With the creation of a separate branch, the crossed arrows were designated for the Special Forces officers. The Special Forces officer branch inherited this insignia from the Indian scouts, several of whom were awarded Medals of Honor for their actions with U.S. forces. The **crossed arrows** were also used by the 1st Special Service Force in World War II. During the 1960s, it was not uncommon to see SF officers sporting the crossed arrows on their uniform collars.

In July of 1983 the **Special Forces Tab** was authorized to be worn by SF qualified personnel. Upon completion of SF training the soldier is authorized to wear the tab on the left shoulder. This tab is worn above the Airborne tab and SF arrowhead. If an individual is also Ranger qualified, he may wear the Ranger tab as well. It would be located between the SF tab and the Airborne tab.

Special Forces engineer sergeants are just as skilled in building bridges as demolishing them. As part of their mission, they may do "nation building" with a hammer and saw as well as C4 and Det-cord. The ODA engineer sergeants perform and instruct in all aspects of combat engineering, light construction, and demolitions techniques. Here an SF engineer sergeant prepares a charge of military dynamite for a training mission. It should be noted that dynamite is not the first explosive of choice; however, SF are taught to use what they have, and in a Third World setting or UW role, this may be the only explosive material available.

to organize, train, advise, direct, and support indigenous military or paramilitary forces in UW and FID operations. The units are capable of training a force up to a battalion in size. Unlike a conventional unit, which will deploy with its full chain of command, staff officers, and support and logistics units, SF does not. The 82nd

does not send an infantry squad out on a mission and say, "By the way, sergeant, it's all yours." On the other hand, that is exactly how an SF ODA deploys; often the SF team is the only U.S. military presence in a country.

The Special Forces ODA is commanded by a captain (18A00). He may also command or advise

Call him "Doc" or "18-Delta," the SF medical sergeant is one of the most capable medical specialists in the U.S. military. He is trained in first aid, trauma care, dentistry, and veterinary skills. He functions as an independent medical care practitioner in a remote environment, and takes care of the A-team's medical needs as well as those of any indigenous personnel. Although he is a medical specialist, the SF 18D is also a combatant. He not only knows how to perform a tracheotomy, he can perform a CAS strike or take out an enemy sentry with the same precision. When the other members of the team head out on a patrol with their LBE and loads, he will also be carrying a medical pack or trauma bag filled with assorted medical supplies.

concert with conventional forces in large-scale operations. As the team leader, he is accountable for everything that happens on that team, right or wrong. He is tasked with mission planning—working with the team specialist to establish the best possible strategy for mission success. As Captain Steve Warman, of ODA-581, 5th SFG(A) sums it up, the team leader "is responsible for the men and their equipment, and makes sure that everything happens the way it is supposed to happen."

When you look at the difference between an SF captain and the captain of a conventional unit,

The two Communications "Commo" Sergeants of the ODA advise the detachment commander on communications matters. They install, operate, and maintain FM, AM, HF, VHF, and SHF radio communications in voice, CW, and burst radio nets. Here SFC Greg Green of the 1st Special Forces Group (Airborne) performs a communications check. He is using an AN/PSC-5 Multi-band, Multi-mission communications terminal, with SatCom antennae.

up to a battalion-size group of indigenous combat troops. He is proficient in those tasks that support the detachment's mission-essential task list, or METL, with knowledge of a broad spectrum of common and special operations tasks. Not only must the SF captain know the skills that will make him mission-capable during independent special operations, he must also be able to operate in

A Special Forces sergeant takes aim with his M4A1/M203. He will be ready to provide cover fire for his team members as they move stealthily through the wooded marsh.

you see the vast chasm in their operational capabilities. A typical infantry, airborne, or armor captain will operate usually within 10 kilometers of his command and control. He'll have full logistical support and medical facilities nearby, and his operations will be in concert with other larger units. His need for E&E skills is limited, and he will normally fight within range of artillery support. Conversely, the SF captain will operate in isolated areas, often over 100 kilometers from his headquarters. Logistical support will be little, if any, and often he'll live off the land; availability for MedEvac is limited and will depend on the team medical specialist. ODAs will operate independently of other units. The need for survival and E&E skills

is high, and the SF captain will rarely operate within the range of friendly fire support.

The executive officer of the ODA is the detachment technician, a warrant officer (WO) (180A0). He serves as second in command, ensuring that the detachment commander's decisions are implemented. His tasks also include administrative and logistical aspects of area studies, briefbacks and operational plans (OPLANs), and operational orders (OPORDs). He will assist in the recruitment of indigenous troops and the subsequent training of these combat forces up to and including a battalion size. In the event the mission requires the ODA to run a "split team op," the WO would command one of these teams.

What makes SF soldiers special? An SF sergeant summed it up best when he said, "You look at his shoulder, that tells you his Quals [Qualifications, e.g. Airborne, Ranger, Special Forces tabs]. You look at his chest, that tells you his schools [e.g. Air Assault, Airborne, EIB (Expert Infantry Badge),etc.]. You look in his eyes, that tells you what kind of a man he is."

The next man on the team is the operations sergeant (18Z50), the "team sergeant." He is the senior NCO on the detachment. A master sergeant, he advises the ODA commander on all training and operational matters. His job also entails providing the team with tactical and technical guidance and support. He will prepare the operations and training portion of the area studies, briefbacks and OPLANs, and OPORDs. In the absence of the WO, the "team sergeant" will fill in this position.

Directing the ODA's intelligence training, collections, analysis and dissemination is the assistant operations and intelligence sergeant (18F40), a sergeant first class (SFC). As the name implies, he assists the operations sergeant in preparing area studies, briefbacks, and so on. He is also responsible for field interrogation of enemy prisoners. He briefs and debriefs SF and indigenous patrols, and will fill in for the ops sgt. when necessary.

The operations and intelligence sergeant comes from the ranks of Special Forces. He will have been on an ODA for some time and will have attended the Advanced Non-Commissioned Officers Course at the NCO Academy, USAJFK-SWC/S at Ft. Bragg.

Next on the team are the two weapons sergeants (18B40) and (18B30), an SFC and staff sergeant (SSG) respectively. They are responsible for the employment of weapons using conventional and UW tactics and techniques. They will train the indigenous troops as well as other team members in the use of small arms (e.g., pistols, rifles, assault weapons), crew-served weapons (e.g., machine guns, mortars), anti-aircraft (e.g., stingers) and anti-tank weapons (e.g., LAW, AT-4). They may assist the operations sergeant, and they can organize, train, advise, and command up to a company-size indigenous force.

Two engineer sergeants (18C40) SFC and (18C30) SSG supervise, lead, plan, perform, and instruct all aspects of combat engineering and light construction. They are knowledgeable in demolitions and improvised munitions. They will plan and perform sabotage operations. As the weapons sergeants, they can organize, train, advise, and command an indigenous force up to a company size.

Two medical sergeants (18D40) SFC and (18D30) SG provide emergency, routine, and long-term medical treatment for the ODA and associated allied or indigenous forces. They will train, advise, and direct detachment members and indigs in emergency medicine and preventive medical care. In the event of a prolonged mission, they will establish a medical facility and are also trained in veterinary care. They are considered physician substitutes and can provide emergency, routine, and long-term medical care for the ODA, allied forces, and host nation personnel. One other unique capability of the SF medical sergeant is that he is fully schooled in the SF skills and is a combatant. As are the other team members, he is capable of training and commanding up to a company-size force.

Finally, the last two members of the ODA are the communications sergeants (18E40) SFC and (18E30) SSG. These two soldiers advise the detachment commander on communications matters. They install, operate, and maintain FM, AM, HF, VHF, and SHF radio communications in voice, CW, and burst radio nets. They prepare the communications portion of briefbacks, OPLANs, and OPORDs. They will train members of the ODA and indigenous personnel in the use and maintenance of the communication equipment. They can advise, train, and command indigenous forces up to a company in size.

According to Major Tom McCullom, SF-PAO, "A SF soldier is a highly skilled, extremely capable soldier, there is very little he as an individual cannot figure out how to do; but as a team, the team is unstoppable, because each SF soldier builds off the others' strengths. The commo sergeant may know everything to know about commo, but may be weak in demolitions; meanwhile the team has an engineering sergeant that knows everything there is to know about demolitions. And he can help out the commo sergeant. . . . A good team does not just do their job and go home at the end of the day, they socialize together, they know each other. Special Forces are a type A personality times three! SF soldiers have a lot of initiative, [and] the ability to think on their own. They've got to be mature enough that when they are on their own they will be making the right decisions."

While conducting an SR mission, the SF soldier may use a ghillie suit to camouflage his position. He will report his observations using the SALUTE method—Size, Activity, Location, Unit, Time, and Equipment. Special Forces also include their proximity to the target. High command will determine what ordnance to use against the target and whether the SF team's position is considered Danger Close.

Members of the 5th Special Forces Groups (Airborne) practice their lethal trade. Here the Ground Mobility Vehicle (GMV) has pulled off the road into a partial defilade position. While the team sergeant mans the Mark 19, 40mm Grenade Machine Gun, other members of the ODA provide 360 degrees of cover fire, if necessary.

Special Forces Missions

Originally created to train and maintain a guerrilla force against communist aggression in Europe, their primary mission in 1952 was that of unconventional warfare. Over the years the geopolitical world has changed and so has the mission of the Special Forces soldier and ODA. Today, the Special Forces comprises five core missions, and while UW is one of them, they are prepared to conduct and execute any of them. These core missions are the following:

Special Reconnaissance (SR), is defined as the reconnaissance and surveillance activity conducted by Special Operations Forces (SOF). Performed by SF teams, this covers the area of HUMINT (HUMan INTelligence), placing U.S. "eyes on target" in hostile, denied, or politically sensitive territory. An SF team could be tasked to conduct these missions. This means putting warm bodies on the ground in a specific location to accomplish what no satellite can do. An ODA performing an SR mission will be infiltrated into enemy area to report back to their commanders necessary information needed to carry out ongoing attacks. Special Forces teams may be utilized to acquire or verify, by visual observation or other methods available, information concerning the capabilities, intentions, and activities of an enemy force. SR may also include the placement of remote sensor equipment in enemy territory. Special Reconnaissance includes recording meteorological, hydrographic, and geographic characteristics of the objective area. Additionally, SR comprises target acquisition, bomb damage assessment, and post-strike reconnaissance. Reconnaissance provides the CinC with intelligence needed to conduct operations.

SR provides intelligence that is *strategic*—data that is required by national decision makers in formulating national or foreign defense policies, *operational*—details and reports used by theater level commanders to plan and conduct their campaigns, and *tactical*—information that commanders need for fighting battles.

Direct Action (DA), involves small-scale offensive actions, normally of a short-term duration conducted by SF teams. Such actions include seizure, destroying, capture of enemy personnel—any action that would inflict damage on enemy personnel or material. Direct action missions may also include the recovery of sensitive items or isolated personnel—e.g., POWs. SF units are highly trained and may employ raids, ambushes, and

Qatar soldiers listen to a class given by SFC Tim Keck of the 5th Special Forces Group (Airborne), on the proper procedures for clearing enemy forces from buildings. *DOD Photo*

A SF captain from ODA 052, 10th Special Forces Group (Airborne) pauses to check his map. Wearing snow camouflage, he blends in well with his surroundings. While some units still have the three-color snow camo, he is wearing the newly issued "All White" camo.

Foreign Internal Defense (FID) is a primary means of providing U.S. military SOF's expertise to other governments in support of their internal defense and developmental efforts. FID is one of the SF's primary peacetime tasks. By providing such training, SOF may eliminate the need to deploy conventional forces in a particular region of the world. Yet by employing SF ODAs in this mission, teams stay prepared for their role as combat advisers in the event of war. FID missions have included basic static line parachute training, MFF, and jumpmaster training; light infantry tactics, encompassing counterinsurgency operations, advance patrolling, urban combat, and advance marksmanship/sniper training; water operations, including riverine ops, small boat ops, and scout swimming; and engineering and communications training. Medical and veterinary training are also incorporated in the SF FID missions.

Unconventional Warfare (UW), the origin of SF, encompasses guerrilla warfare, the use of irregular forces—normally indigenous personnel operating in enemy-held territory—and other direct offensive, low visibility, covert, or clandestine operations. Incorporated in the UW mission are the indirect activities of subversion, sabotage, intelligence gathering, and evasion and escape nets. Armed rebellion against an established force or occupying power is often within the scope of UW. In wartime, Special Forces may be tasked with directly supporting any resistance or guerrilla force. This is commonly accomplished by infiltrating operational detachments or A-teams into denied or sensitive areas for the purpose of training, equipping and advising, or directing indigenous forces.

Counterterrorism (CT) consists of the offensive actions taken to prevent, deter, and respond to terrorism; this includes intelligence gathering and threat analysis. SF troops are ideal for engaging in antiterrorism and counterterrorism missions. Such assets could be on station in the rapidly changing environment of a CT operation,

other small unit tactics in the pursuit of these mission goals. They may employ mines and other demolitions or conduct attacks by employing fire support from air, ground, or sea assets. Direct action may employ stand-off weapons, such as a sniper team or an SF team with a SOFLAM (Special Operation Force Laser Acquisition Marker) who lase a target for terminal guidance ordnance—e.g., precision-guided "smart bombs."

Although one of the five core missions of Special Forces, CT, or Counterterrorism, is not talked about openly by USASOC. They do not want to give the terrorist any edge. This member of a CT team is "armed for bear"; he carries the M4A1 carbine with dual magazine, vertical grip and sight, a Berretta M9 pistol, flash-bang grenades, and numerous ammo magazines at the ready. He wears special head and eye protection.

greatly enhancing flexibility in meeting the critical demands of the situation. The CT mission could include training of host nation counterterrorist forces, conducting hostage rescues, recovering sensitive material from terrorists, or performing DA on the terrorist infrastructure to reduce the effects of international or state-sponsored terrorist activities.

Collateral Missions

Due to the nature of SF soldiers, who can adapt, overcome, and improvise according to ever-changing missions and environments, they are frequently called upon to perform Collateral Activities, in addition to the five core missions.

These activities include **Humanitarian Assistance**, as in Operation Provide Comfort (the highly trained medical specialists in SF are often called for such missions); **Security Assistance**, training and advisory roles; Personnel Recovery, from **Combat Search and Rescue** (CSAR) to **Non-Combatant Operations** (NEOs), such as Operation Assure Lift in Sierra Leone, where members of 3rd SFG(A) extracted Ambassador Ann Wright from her embassy in 1997; **Counter-Drug (CD)** efforts, supporting counter drug operations inside the United States in cooperation with JTF-6 and in various locations OCONUS (OutsideCONtinental US); and **Counter Mine**, conducting several demining initiatives worldwide. The United States is the world leader in removing mines, and the SOF and SF lead this initiative. Finally, there is the area of **Special Activities**, which is classified.

CHAPTER 6

Selection and Training

In addition to the active and National Guard SF groups, two additional groups come under the command of USASOC. They are the U.S. Army John F. Kennedy Special Warfare Center and School (Airborne) and U.S. Army Special Warfare Training Group (Airborne). These two groups are tasked with the training of the Special Forces soldiers. Their mission is to assess, select, train, and qualify Special Forces soldiers in preparation for assignment to an Operational Detachment-Alpha, or ODA.

The JFK Special Warfare Center and School is responsible for special operations training, leader development, doctrine, and personnel advocacy. The center and school's training group conduct the full spectrum of training in special operations. The 1st Battalion administers Special Forces Assessment and Selection (SFAS) and the SF Qualification Course, or Q-Course. The 2nd Battalion is responsible for advanced SF skills, military free fall (MFF); combat diving (SCUBA); the SERE (Survival, Escape, Resistance, and Evasion) course; Special Operations Target Interdiction course; Special Forces Advanced Reconnaissance, Target Analysis & Exploitation Techniques course, and Advanced Special Operations Techniques. The 3rd Battalion teaches civil affairs, psychological operations, Special Forces warrant officers, language training, and regional area studies.

What makes an SF soldier special? What makes him stand head and shoulders above any other soldier in the world? He is in a class by himself. He is a mature, highly skilled, outstandingly trained individual, and without a doubt the finest unconventional warfare expert in the world, bar none. He is a teacher, a fighter, and oftentimes a diplomat. And a warrior of uncommon physical and mental caliber, ready to serve at a moment's notice anywhere his mission may take him. An SF sergeant summed it up best when he said, "You look at his shoulder, that tells you his QUALs [Qualifications, e.g. Airborne, Ranger, Special Forces tabs]. You look at his chest, that tells you his schools [e.g., MFF, SCUBA,

Land navigation is an essential skill for SF soldiers. While they are well versed in the use of high tech gear, like the Global Positioning System (GPS), they are just as comfortable with a map and compass. The SF soldier will use whatever means are available, even if that means navigating from the stars.

The subdued patch of the John F. Kennedy Special Warfare Center and School. This instructor is also Ranger and SF qualified.

"Airborne, All The Way!" All members of the U.S. Army Special Forces are Airborne qualified. This training takes place at the U.S. Army Airborne School, Ft. Benning, Georgia. Upon successful completion, a soldier is awarded the "Silver Wings" and is no longer considered a Low Energy Ground soldier, or "LEG."

Pathfinder, and so on]. You look in his eyes, that tells you what kind of a man he is."

One of the unique characteristics making the Special Forces "special" is the fact that soldiers who make it into this branch of the Army are triple volunteers. First, an individual must volunteer for service with the U.S. Army. Second, they volunteer for Airborne training. Then, after serving in their Military Occupational Specialty (MOS), they volunteer for Special Forces. When the time comes for the SFAS, the soldier has a couple years under his belt. This ensures that SF

soldiers are well grounded in conventional Army tactics before undergoing Special Forces training.

During the 1970s and early 1980s, an individual could enlist directly into the SF field. He would go through Basic Combat Training, Advanced Individual Training, Airborne School and then go on for Special Forces training. Today, the SF "direct" enlistment option is no longer available. Special Forces is a "non-accession" branch of the Army, which means SF does not accept entry-level personnel. Any male soldier may volunteer for SFAS. At this point he

Where the journey into SF begins—the Special Forces Assessment and Selection phase at Camp MacKall. The purpose of SFAS is to identify soldiers who have the potential for Special Forces training.

The SF weapons sergeants are trained on more than 80 weapons—U.S. and foreign, friend and foe, old and new. You never know what weapons the host nation will be using, so you train up on everything you can get your hands on. Brass flies into the air as two members of ODA-173, "The Sea Pigs," send some .45 caliber rounds down range using the M3 submachine gun, also known as the "Grease Gun." A World War II–era weapon, it is still in use today.

may not be Airborne qualified. If he makes it through SFAS, he will have to go through Airborne training before entering the Qualification Course.

To join Special Forces the soldier must be a proven performer, having risen to the rank of captain or sergeant. Warrant officers come out of the SF senior NCO ranks. Here is the training progression, beginning with Airborne, SFAS, and then the Q-Course.

Airborne

The separation of the SF trooper from his fellow soldiers begins in the hot Georgia sun. Airborne training for the prospective Special Forces trooper is conducted at the U.S. Army Airborne School at Ft. Benning, Georgia. For the next three weeks he will be at the mercy of the Army's "Black Hats," the Airborne instructors of the 1st Battalion (Airborne), 507th Parachute Infantry Regiment, who will convert a "leg" into an "Airborne" trooper. He will learn what it takes to hurl oneself out of an airplane for the purpose of infiltrating into his mission drop zone (DZ). And he will run.

He will also learn a new mantra, which he will repeat over and over during the three weeks at Ft. Benning. He will shout out, "Motivated! Motivated!! Motivated!!! Airborne!" and he will run. He will repeat the mantra, "Fired up! Fired up!! Fired up!!! Airborne!" and when his body is aching and cannot move another inch, he will run some more. These veteran Airborne qualified instructors wearing the "Black Hats" ensure these potential Green Berets are indeed motivated and fired up! This is far more than an evolution. This is Airborne!

Basic airborne training is broken into segments of a week each: Ground, Tower, and Jump Week.

SF Engineers receive extensive training in building and construction. Often, nation building is accomplished with a hammer and saw rather than an M4A1 and Claymore. There are times, of course, when what has gone up must now come down. It has been said that most problems can be solved with the proper amount of high explosives. Here an SF engineer sergeant is preparing a timing fuse for an explosive charge.

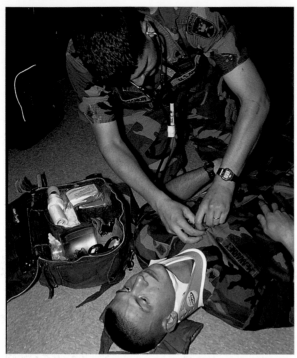

The Special Forces medical sergeants training is one of the most exhaustive training programs in the SF/SOF arena. Very often the SF medic will be the only source of medical care to which the team or indigenous personnel have access. He is trained and capable of serving as a physician substitute in the austere environments where the Operational Detachment-Alpha (ODA) operate.

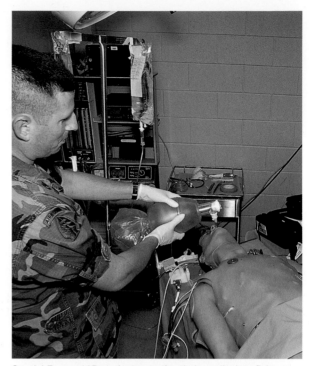

Special Forces 18D students practice their medical proficiency on the Human Patient Simulator. This highly sophisticated simulator, in use at the JSOMTC, is capable of producing normal and abnormal physiological responses to myriad anesthetic, medical, and surgical events. Lungs fill with and empty of air, eyes can become fixed and dilated, and so on. The benefit of the simulator is that these conditions are repeatable, thus removing a variable in the restoration or demise of the patient. By using the patient simulator, there is no risk to live patients during this phase of training.

During Ground Week, our trainee will start an intensive program of instruction designed to prepare the trooper to complete his parachute jump. He will learn how to execute a flawless parachute landing fall (PLF) to land safely in the landing zone (LZ). The PLF uses five points of contact designed to absorb the shock of landing and distribute it across the balls of the feet, calves, thighs, buttocks, and the push-up muscles of the back. He will learn the proper way to exit an aircraft using mockups of a C-130 and a C-141. He will climb up a 34-foot tower, where he will be connected to the lateral drift apparatus and upon command will assume door position and jump. Proper body position will be evaluated, and he'll do it over and over until the "Black Hats" are happy; and he will run.

Next comes Tower Week. Now that our trainee has learned how to exit, position, and land, he will have this second week to refine those skills. Using a training device known as the swing landing tower (SLT), where he is hooked up to a parachute harness, he jumps from a 12-foot-high elevated platform. The apparatus provides downward motion and oscillation to simulate an actual parachute jump. To make things more challenging for the student, the instructors have control of the SLT and can determine if they want to land him hard or soft. As one student rushes toward the ground, hands clinging to his harness, the instructor yells at him, "Hazard left!" and leans into the rope controlling the drop. He watches as the airborne trainee hits the ground, and he had better land in a manner to avoid the imaginary obstacle, or the "airborne sergeant" will have a few choice words for him and a number of pushups, too. During week two the student gets to ride the "tower." The tower is designed to give the student practice in controlling his parachute during the descent from 250 feet, and in executing a PLF upon landing. He will learn how to handle parachute malfunctions, and he will run.

Finally, week three, Jump Week. The potential SF trooper will perform five parachute jumps. First, an individual jump with a T-10B parachute. Next a mass exit with equipment and T-10B chute; then another individual exit with MC1-1B parachute and tactical assembly. His fourth jump will be a mass exit at night with a T-10B and tactical equipment. And finally the fifth jump is either an individual jump with an MV1-1B, or a mass jump with a T-10B parachute.

The United States Army's "Guide for Airborne Students" states, "Airborne training is a rite of passage for the warrior." Upon graduation he will be awarded the coveted Silver Wings and is now qualified as an airborne trooper.

Special Forces Assessment and Selection (SFAS)

What is SFAS? The purpose of SFAS is to identify soldiers who have the potential for Special Forces training. The career management

Adapt, Overcome, and Improvise is the hallmark of an SF soldier. The SF Commo Sergeant is instructed in numerous communications devices, from the basic Morse code to high-tech satellite communications. Here is an improvised radio antenna. It has been built with branches, 550 cord, spoons from a Meal Ready to Eat (MRE) and commo wire. It may seem crude, but it works. Want to be more creative? One ODA has practiced using a kite get an antenna aloft; now that is thinking outside the box!

field (CMF) 18 includes positions concerned with the employment of highly specialized elements to accomplish specifically directed missions in times of peace and war. Many of these missions are conducted at times when employment of conventional military forces is not feasible or is not considered in the best interests of the United States. Training for and participation in these missions is strenuous, somewhat hazardous, and often sensitive in nature. For these reasons it is a prerequisite that every prospective Special Forces soldier successfully complete the 24-day SFAS program. SFAS is conducted by the 1st Battalion, 1st SWTG(A) at Rowe Training Facility, Camp MacKall, approximately an hour's drive from Ft. Bragg.

The SFAS program assesses and selects soldiers for attendance at the Special Forces Qualification Course (SFQC). This program allows SF an opportunity to assess each soldier's capabilities by testing his physical, emotional, and mental stamina. SFAS also allows each soldier the opportunity to make a meaningful and educated decision about SF and his career plan. Any male soldier may volunteer for SFAS. A normal progression will see a number of RANGERs volunteer; however, a large portion comes from soldiers with varying MOSs.

Applicants volunteering for SFAS must meet the following criteria: male soldier in rank of E-4 to E-7; U.S. citizen with a high school diploma or GED (General Education Development certificate); airborne qualified, or a volunteer for airborne training (candidates not airborne qualified will be scheduled for airborne training at the completion of SFAS); able to swim 50 meters wearing boots and battle dress uniform (BDU); meeting Special Forces fitness standards; eligible for a "Secret" security clearance; and not a prior Airborne or SF voluntary terminee.

All candidates participate in a variety of activities designed to place them under various forms of physical and mental stress. The training assesses potential and qualities through behavioral observation, and analysis of performance measures and recorded data. All tasks are performed with limited information and no performance feedback. What this means is no praise, no encouragement, no harassment; tasks are assigned and rated, period. SFAS assesses a candidate's potential for being independent, yet a team player and a leader. Instructors look for the soldiers to demonstrate the following individual attributes: motivation, accountability, maturity, stability, teamwork, intelligence, physical fitness and trustworthiness. Leadership traits include communications, influence, judgment, decisiveness, and responsibility.

The SFAS program has two phases. Phase one assesses physical fitness, motivations, and the ability to cope with stress. Activities during this phase include psychological tests, physical fitness and swim tests, runs, obstacle course, basic First Aid, land navigation, ruckmarches, and military orienteering exercises. An evaluation board meets after the first phase to determine which of the candidates will be allowed to continue the program. The second phase assesses leadership and teamwork skills. SFAS not only serves to select the proper soldier for Special Forces training, it screens out those individuals who are lacking the qualities and potential to complete training. Only those soldiers who have demonstrated the potential to complete Special Forces training successfully are allowed to continue. At the end of the 24 days, another board meets to select those soldiers who may attend the SFQC. Fewer than 50 percent of the soldiers that start SFAS are selected for Special Forces training.

After a soldier is selected through SFAS, he will return to his unit and wait for his slot in the SFQC. This process may take several months before the soldier will actually begin SF training. Those soldiers selected for MOS 18B (weapons) and MOS 18C (engineer) report directly to Ft. Bragg to begin their training. Soldiers selected for MOS 18E (communications) will first complete a course in Advance International Morse Code (AIMC) before attending the SFQC.

SFQC and SFDOQC (Special Forces Detachment Officer Qualification Course)

Each branch of service that produces special operations personnel has its own unique training. This specialized training not only emphasizes physical prowess and military skills, but also serves to bring about teamwork, unit cohesiveness, and esprit de corps. For the U.S. Air Force's Special Tactics Teams, it is accomplished with Indoctrination and the Pipeline; for the U.S. Navy SEALs it is achieved with BUD/S and "Hell Week." For the Special Forces soldier it is the "Q-Course."

The SFQC/SFDOQC teaches and develops the skills necessary for effective use of the SF soldier. Duties in CMF 18 primarily involve participation in Special Operations interrelated fields of unconventional warfare. These include foreign internal defense and direct action missions as part of a small operations team or ODA. Duties at other levels involve command, control, and support functions. Frequently, duties require regional orientation, including foreign language training and in-country experience. SF emphasizes not only unconventional tactics, but also knowledge of nations in waterborne, desert, jungle, mountain, or Arctic operations.

The CMF 18 is subdivided into five accession MOS: detachment commander -18A; SF weapons sergeant - 18B; SF engineer sergeant - 18C; SF medical sergeant - 18D; and SF communications sergeant - 18E. Each SF volunteer receives extensive training in a specialty, which prepares him for his future assignment in an SF unit. SF units are designed to operate either unilaterally or in support of and combined with native military and paramilitary forces. Levels of employment for Special Operations Forces include advising and assisting host governments, involvement in continental United States–based training, and direct participation in combat operations.

After successful completion of SFAS, officers who have not already attended their Advance Course will attend either the Infantry or Armor Officer Advance Course. For the enlisted soldier, the SFQC is currently divided into three phases. Phase I is Individual Skills, Phase II is MOS Qualification, and Phase III is Collective Training. The enlisted applicant's SFQC training will be scheduled upon successful completion of SFAS.

Phase I—Individual Skills

During this time, soldiers in process are trained on common skills for CMF 18, skill level three. Training is 40 days long and is taught at the Camp Rowe Training Facility. The training covered during this phase includes land navigation (cross-country) and small unit tactics. This phase culminates with a special operations overview.

Phase II—MOS (Military Operation Specialty) Qualification

For the enlisted soldier, the decision on which of the four specialties he will receive training in will be made based upon his background, aptitude, and desire, and the needs of Special Forces. Training for this phase is 65 days and culminates with a mission planning cycle. During this phase, soldiers are trained in their different specialties:

18A - SF detachment commander. Training includes teaching the officer student the planning and leadership skills he will need to direct and employ other members of his detachment. He will be trained in escape and recovery; infiltration (Infil) and extraction (Exfil) techniques; SF weapons, engineering, medical and communications skills; Military Decision Making Process, MDMP; terrain analysis; Direct Action; Special

Reconnaissance; Foreign Internal Defense; and Unconventional Warfare. Training is conducted at Fort Bragg, North Carolina, and is 24 weeks long. The culmination of this training is an FTX called the Troy Trek, held in the Pisgah National Forest or at Ft. A.P. Hill.

18B - SF weapons sergeant. Training includes learning the characteristics and capabilities of more than 89 types of U.S. and foreign light weapons—e.g., handguns, submachine guns, rifles, machine guns, mortars, anti-tank weapons, and man-portable air defense weapons. The trainee will learn range planning, tactics, indirect fire operations, weapons emplacement, and integrated combined arms fire control planning. He will learn how to teach marksmanship and the employment of weapons to others. Training is conducted at Fort Bragg, North Carolina, for 24 weeks.

18C - SF engineer sergeant. Training includes planning and constructing buildings, bridges, and field fortifications, as well as the use of demolitions for their destruction. The trainee learns how to read blueprints, as well as developing carpentry, electrician, and plumbing skills. Training also includes target analysis and demolitions techniques, including electric and non-electric firing systems. He will be taught the latest demolitions techniques and how to improvise with substitutes for ammunition and explosives. Training also includes land mine warfare and de-mining techniques. The program is conducted at Fort Bragg, North Carolina, for 24 weeks.

18D - SF medical sergeant. This course also includes U.S. Navy SEAL corpsmen, U.S. Army Ranger medics, and U.S. Air Force pararescuemen. The medical training is divided into two portions. First, trainees go through the Special Operations Combat Medic course (SOMC). Upon successful completion of this program, they move on to the more advanced Special Forces Medical Sergeants course.

At the SOMC, which lasts 24 weeks, the soldiers undergo a curriculum of concentrated medical training specifically designed for special operations medical personnel. They receive emergency medical technician-basic (EMT-B) and paramedic (EMT-P) training and certification. They also get certified by the American Heart Association in basic life support and advanced cardiac life support. SOMC training teaches students how to manage trauma patients prior to evacuation and provide them with medical treatment. This includes minor field surgery, pharmacology, combat trauma management, advanced airway treatment, and military evacuation procedures. Students will actually be assigned to hands-on patient care both in emergency and hospital settings as part of their training. This is conducted during a four-week assignment in one of the country's largest metropolitan areas, New York City.

The second major phase of this program is the Special Forces Medical Sergeants Course Training. This course provides skills in trauma management, infectious disease, cardiac care, life support, basic dentistry, basic Veterinary skills, X-ray, anesthesia, surgical procedures, team medical care, and indigenous population care. Training is conducted at the Joint Special Operations Medical Training Center located at Fort Bragg, North Carolina. Training takes approximately 57 weeks.

18E - SF communications sergeant. The purpose of this course is to train and qualify the SF soldier in the basic skills and knowledge required to perform duties as the SF communications sergeant on a Special Forces ODA. Training includes AIMC—encompassing instruction in radio telegraph procedures, military block printing, and exercises in transmitting and receiving Morse code; cryptographic systems; burst outstation systems; and common radios found throughout the Army. Students become familiar with antenna theory and radio wave propagation

78

continued on page 82

Just east of John F. Kennedy Hall, Fort Bragg, North Carolina, behind a tall fence topped with barbed wire, is the U.S. Army Joint Special Operations Medical Training Center (JSOMTC). Here, the 18-Deltas, or Special Forces Medics, learn their trade. This facility is responsible for the training of all enlisted medical personnel within the United States Special Operations Command. Over a decade in development, the JSOMTC is the result of an effort to create a single medical training facility for all Special Operations Forces (SOF) enlisted medical personnel. The JSOMTC was created for the centralized training of Special Forces medics, the Special Forces Medical Sergeants Course (SFMSC), and a new training program for all non-SF SOF medics, called the Special Operations Combat Medic Course (SOCM). With all SOF enlisted medical personnel now training at a single site, and with all becoming certified EMT-Paramedics, the level of medical training and of medical interoperability within SOF has been significantly enhanced.

According to LTC. Clifford Cloonan of JSOMTC, this Department of Defense (DOD) training center was established to consolidate and standardize medical training among all DOD SOF, while continuing a mission to provide first-class medical training to U.S. Army Special Forces (SF) medics (18D). Beginning in 1986, in an effort to consolidate enlisted medical training for all DOD SOF, the headquarters of the United States Special Operations Command (USSOCOM) and the U.S. Army Medical Department Center and School, began preliminary discussions on the feasibility of integrating Special Operations medical training in a single facility at Fort Bragg, North Carolina. The training of Special Forces medics had formerly been divided between programs at

Fort Sam Houston and Fort Bragg and there existed no specialized advanced medical training for non-SF special operations medics, e.g. Rangers, SEALS, and USAF Para-rescue. In 1996 the JSOMTC was open for business.

The expected benefits were improved training for non-SF SOF medical personnel (who were formerly trained only to the conventional force standard), reduced training costs, and standardization of all SOF medical training leading to enhanced interoperability. Early in the process of designing the joint SOF medic training program to be taught at this new facility, it was decided that training and certification as a paramedic to National Registry EMT-Paramedic standards would be an integral and requisite part of the course.

This new training center uses the latest training techniques and technological advances to impart medical skills and knowledge to SOF medical personnel. The JSOMTC is designed to support the training of multiple classes simultaneously. Located on 9.6 acres of land, the 74,000-square-foot main building houses the offices, classrooms, and ancillary facilities necessary to support training. There are 17 large and small classrooms available for small group sessions and lecture, the largest of these capable of seating 200 students. Additionally, there are more than two acres of enclosed woodlands on the grounds of the JSOMTC to support training in simulated field environments.

A barracks facility constructed near the JSOMTC houses 140 single and unaccompanied students and an identical barracks is currently under construction immediately adjacent to the existing barracks. Upon completion of the second barracks all single and unaccompanied students will reside within immediate proximity to the JSOMTC.

A host of other facilities dedicated to instruction for the SF & SOF medical specialist are located within the JSOMTC. Ten operative procedure rooms modeled after modern hospital operating rooms are equipped for instruction in surgical techniques. Two 800-square-foot laboratory classrooms are available for student instruction and can accommodate up to 48 students each. These laboratories would be the envy of contemporary university facilities, each having a five-headed microscope with mounted digital camera. A modern anatomy and physiology teaching laboratory is well equipped for instruction. A dedicated x-ray suite is available for teaching radiological techniques with field x-ray equipment. These specialized areas are supported by a large medical logistics division complete with instrument sterilization equipment and supply storage areas. Between five and eight cadaver specimens are available for each class through arrangement with a local university. In addition to the "specimens," JSOMTC has a state-of-the-art patient simulator. This sophisticated computer patient can be programmed with an assortment of maladies that the student must identify and treat properly. It simulates all the correct body responses—eyes dilate, chest rises and falls, it can be intubated, IVs can be administered to it, or it can be charged "back to life."

Funding obtained from USSOCOM in 1998 allowed for the creation, within the JSOMTC, of an SOF-focused medical library and a student computer lab. The JSOMTC currently has holdings of more than 700 titles covering a wide range of topics of relevance to SOF medicine. In addition to books, the library subscribes to a variety of medical journals of SOF relevance, and has videotapes that can be viewed in the library. The 1,300-square-foot library allows for approximately 40 patrons to sit and study. Students can facilitate their learning on interactive CDs and via the Internet at 44 state-of-the-art computer work stations located in the library and in a separate computer lab. Access to MEDLINE and other full-text databases allows patrons to read the latest journals in the field and search for relevant articles of interest.

Special Forces medical specialists often have to deal with animals of the region. For this purpose there is also a 9,000-square-foot veterinary facility that supports veterinary and medical skills training. Complete with automated feeding equipment and air exchange mechanisms, this facility incorporates the newest animal care provisions and emulates the finest facilities of this type in the country. The latest in computer, electronic, and fiber optic technology has been incorporated into the design of the JSOMTC.

Instruction at the JSOMTC is provided by a skilled and experienced group of permanently assigned officers and enlisted personnel from all branches of the military. Dean of the JSOMTC is a colonel army physician with a special operations background. The Navy and the Air Force each provide an assistant dean with medical, educational, and special operations training and experience. Day-to-day operation of the facility is the responsibility of the Special Operations Medical Training Battalion, which is commanded by a lieutenant colonel Special Forces branch officer. Included in the staff are officers selected for their professional expertise and special operations experience from the Medical, Dental, Veterinary, Nursing, and Physician Assistant branches. Enlisted instructors are assigned from SOF in the Army, Navy, and Air Force. Enlisted technicians specializing in pharmacy, radiology, laboratory diagnostics, surgery, animal care, and logistics and personnel management provide additional support. A group of civilian employees with backgrounds in education, personnel management, information management, and pre-hospital emergency medical care complete the staff of the JSOMTC.

U.S. Army Special Forces students attend the 46-week Special Forces Medical Sergeants (SFMS) course, which is Phase II of a three-phase, 58-week-long Special Forces Qualification Course conducted at Ft. Bragg. Students in this course must successfully complete the 24-week SOCM curriculum before continuing on for an additional 22 weeks of specialized training in medical, surgical, dental, veterinary, and preventive medicine subjects. Upon completion of this course, students are qualified to function as independent health care providers. USN personnel qualified for this advanced training attend a similar course of instruction at the JSOMTC, known as the Advanced Special Operations Combat Medic course (ADSOCM), which is also 22 weeks in length. Upon completion of this course, the Navy awards these students the title of Independent Duty Corpsman (IDC).

Joint Special Operations Medical Training Center, Ft. Bragg, North Carolina.

In addition to the four weeks of clinical training provided during the SOCM portion of their training, U.S. Army SFMS and USN ADSOCM students receive another four weeks of clinical experience (called Special Operations Clinical Training, or SOCT) at selected military health care facilities throughout the eastern and central United States. During this rotation, the students will perform ride-alongs with city EMS units and serve in the emergency rooms of various metropolitan hospitals.

The JSOMTC participates in the continuing medical education or medical sustenance training of SOF medical personnel in numerous ways. Qualified Special Forces Medical sergeants receive two weeks of medical instruction at the JSOMTC as part of their Advanced Non-Commissioned Officers Course. Advanced Cardiac Life Support Instructor certification is available to qualified personnel through JSOMTC-taught instruction. Qualified SOF medical personnel may also attend Advanced Trauma Life Support courses that are conducted periodically by the Defense Medical Readiness Training Institute using JSOMTC facilities. In addition, a number of initiatives are being pursued that will provide JSOMTC instruction via distance learning to SOF medical personnel worldwide. In the near future, SOF personnel will be able to continue their medical education or receive support in the field by logging on to a JSOMTC World Wide Web home page via the Internet.

Currently, the JSOMTC is tasked with the execution of two complete courses of instruction, the SFMS, and the SOCM. Also provided is instruction for two modular courses, the USAF EMT-I course for Air Force Pararescue (PJs) not assigned to a special operations unit, and the USN ADSOCM for senior SEAL corpsmen. In addition, portions of two other Special Warfare Center and School Courses, the 18D Special Forces Medic Advanced Non-Commissioned Officer Course and the Special Forces officer orientation course, are also taught at the JSOMTC.

and learn how to teach these skills to others. They will be taught how to install, operate, and maintain FM, AM, HF, VHF, UHF, and SHF communications in voice, continuous wave, and burst radio nets, and learn SF communication operations procedures and techniques. Training culminates with an around-the-world communications field training exercise called Maxgain. Training is conducted at Ft. Bragg, North Carolina, and Camp Gruber, Oklahoma, and lasts 32 weeks.

Phase III - Collective Training

The third and final phase of the SFQC is a 38-day training period conducted at Camp MacKall. Soldiers are instructed in Special Operations, Direct Action, Isolation, Mission Planning, Air Operations (LZ/DZ, MPU, Resupply), and Unconventional Warfare (UW) training. In collective training all the instruction, hard work, and preparation come together. This field training exercise combines and strengthens both the specialty training and common skills. Soldiers from each of the SF skills areas and a detachment commander will put their training to the test. Approximately 160–170 students form 10–12 "A-teams," or ODAs. These ODAs will vary in size ranging from as few as eight to as many as 15 students.

The ODAs will be deployed as separate teams throughout the Uwaharrie National Forest for a UW exercise. Each of the ODAs will have a Training Group cadre member who will be their evaluator for their "final exam." This exercise comes complete with some 120 opposing force (Op Force) soldiers, a guerrilla force (Gs) numbering around 200, and a civilian auxiliary. The students will have to work with the guerrilla force just as they would in a real-world situation. While the SF and Gs are learning to deal with each other, they are being hunted and often attacked by OpForce troopers. This exercise will last for two weeks and is known as Robin Sage.

Robin Sage

The Robin Sage exercise takes place in the fictional country of Pineland on the continent of Atlantica, located in the Atlantic Ocean between America and Europe. Surrounding Pineland are OpForLand, DozerLand, and NeutraState. Pineland is of strategic importance to the United States. For this reason, members of the 9th Special Forces Group (Airborne), also a fictitious unit, have been tasked to provide military assistance. The guerrilla forces have been fighting for some time. The ODA-914 of 9th Group will be sent in to establish a link with these forces and train them in UW techniques.

Depending on their mission profiles, the student ODAs will be inserted by helicopter, parachute, boat, or truck. Regardless of how the team infils, it will ultimately be humping a ruck through some of the roughest terrain in the state of North Carolina, that is, Pineland.

After a day or two, depending on the scenario and how good the team is, the men will make contact with the guerrilla force. If they thought humping an 80–100 pound rucksack for a day or so was rough, it's nothing compared to the task ahead, meeting the guerrilla chief.

The G chief is played by an experienced SF soldier, usually a senior NCO, or perhaps a retired SF soldier brought in to test the mettle of these students who seek to join their ranks. These people know their business and will not spare the fledgling team, or their detachment commander. Whereas the Navy Seals' BUD/S "Hell Week" involves a week of sleep deprivation and 90 percent physical effort, Robin Sage is a thinking man's game.

The ODAs will meet and have to deal with a number of different scenarios and the G's. During their initial meeting, the guerrillas and their leaders are instructed to give the A-team a hard time, to be aloof, stand-offish, perhaps even a little hostile or threatening. One guerrilla comments to

Phase III—Robin Sage. Here is where all the training comes together. The SF students are matched up into functional A–teams, or ODAs, and sent into Pineland. Here they will put to use the skills set they have learned, and discover whether they have what it takes to wear the green beret.

the student, "We have been fighting for years. How much combat do you have? None? How can you tell me how to fight?" One of the G chiefs does not like officers, so he will only deal with the senior NCO of the team. This throws a definite curve to the team and can be unsettling to a detachment commander with too big an ego. When another team meets the G's, the chief's right-hand man is not happy with the situation and tries to convince the ODA to overthrow the chief. These are the types of mind games the G chief and the Gs will force upon the team—and some of these G's take this role-playing very seriously. This sense of realism adds to the intensity of the exercise, and an ODA only has to spend a few days in the base camp before beginning to believe that he really is in Pineland.

Time is a factor, however, since Robin Sage lasts only two weeks. Unless the team really

The team leader of ODA914 converses with the resident guerrilla chief. The G Chief is played by an SF sergeant with many years of experience under his belt. He will ensure that the young captain and his team receive the "Pineland" experience.

Five-Star accommodations, à la SF. While running the Phase III-Robin Sage exercise, this is about as good as it gets—a poncho on the ground and one hanging overhead. "Hey, where is the concierge? My MRE is cold!"

messes up, the Gs will eventually warm to them. Now the team will place into action what they have learned. The weapons specialist will teach the guerrillas how to establish a defensive perimeter around the base camp, the medics will teach hygiene and first aid. The engineers will teach the Gs how to build, and how to take down a target with a very large boom, while the commo specialist provides instruction on radio equipment and procedures. The trainees teach the guerillas small unit tactics, raids, and ambushes. By teaching and doing, the students will learn the hallmarks of a successful raid: Surprise, Speed, and Violence of Action.

Slowly the Gs will evolve from a ragtag bunch of individuals into an organized fighting force. Missions will be planned and executed, all under the watchful eye of the Training Group evaluator. This evaluator is a cadre member of the 1st Special Warfare Training Groups (Airborne). After one such mission, an assault on an OpForce position, the evaluator will sit down with the student and go over his performance. Did you perform the proper Warning Order? It's 98 degrees out here, why didn't you instruct your squad to carry more water? Did you do a recon of the target? Why didn't you wear any face camo? Did you have an alternate plan if you got compromised?

Q-Course student goes over a mission plan with one of the Gs. The hallmarks of a successful raid are surprise, speed, and violence of action on the target. The prospective SF soldier will explain these traits to this guerrilla prior to an assault.

On and on the questions go, and the evaluator will mark the progress or lack of progress of a student. All of these evaluations will go into a leadership assessment that will be used to determine whether the student has what it takes to be a member of the Special Forces.

Trainees must also respect and employ the skills of others on the "island." The OpForce includes soldiers from active military units who have been tasked to assault or engage the team from time to time. The Gs usually possess a modest form of infantry skills, as well as those of clerks, cooks, truck drivers, and so on. The third group who makes up the population of Pineland

During the two weeks of Robin Sage, the SF students get numerous opportunities to apply their skills and exercise their talents. Here a medical sergeant student administers an IV to one of the Gs suffering from heat exhaustion.

Engineer Sergeant student Joe Ferris prepares timing fuses for a future mission. Note that in training, as in combat, his M4A1 carbine is close by, should the need arise. Even in the relative safety of the G Camp, the SF students may come under attack from the OpForce troops at any time.

are the Auxiliary. These are civilian players who for the most part remain anonymous. They offer their homes or barns as "safe houses" for the ODA and Gs; they may provide transportation for a mission, or perhaps bring in some good old home cooking for the freedom fighters of Pineland. Along with the G's supporters, there are those who support the OpForce—e.g., the local sheriff may see the unfamiliar face of an ODA member surveying a target, and lock him up. These local people of the Auxiliary have been assisting in the Robin Sage exercise since the 1960s; indeed, they add a sense of realism to missions.

The exercise ends with a final mission: The ODA has trained the Gs, and they now take on an OpForce target. At this point, Robin Sage is over. The teams will return to Camp MacKall, clean their weapons, gear, and themselves, and await the results of the exercise.

As the evaluations come in, the students are notified whether they have passed or failed the Q-Course. Depending on the recommendation of the evaluators and cadre, a student who does not pass may be recycled for another chance, or he may be dropped. Those who are dropped are sent back to their units.

According the mission brief of the 1st SWTG(A), the soldier who passes will, "Thrive on ambiguity and uncertainty. Think the unconventional and dare the uncommon. Overcome obstacles and persevere when others fail. Adapt to his surroundings and anticipate changes. [He is] physically rugged, morally straight and thoroughly lethal. Triumphs through genius as well as force of arms. [And] immerses himself in the art, science and history of war." Those soldiers who have made it through the course will become members of the U.S. Army Special Forces. They will attend a regimental dinner where they will receive the Special Forces tab, and the coveted green beret. The following day will be the official graduation ceremony from the Q-Course.

Throughout the two weeks of the Robin Sage exercise, the student ODAs will be evaluated on every nuance of their training. Here a Pineland evaluator writes up an "eval" of one of the students following a raid on an OpFor installation.

Every SF Soldier goes through language training. Here members of the 7th Special Forces Group (Airborne) are studying Spanish. Their instructor, who may be from Mexico or South America, is a native speaker. SF soldiers may also learn via computer self-paced training, and from members of the ODA.

The training does not stop here. One of the qualifications of the Special Forces since its inception was that the soldier be conversant in a foreign language. Our newly "tabbed" soldier will now attend language training. Depending on which SF group the soldier will be assigned to, he will be trained in Spanish, French, Portuguese, German, Czech, Polish, Russian, Persian-Farsi, Tagalog, Thai, Vietnamese, Korean, or Modern Standard Arabic.

This training ranges from 17 to 23 weeks, depending on the language. The training stresses basic communications skills with an emphasis on military terminology. Language skills are taught by an instructor indigenous to that country—e.g., the Thai instructor is from Thailand, and the Russian teacher is from Russia, and so on. This assists the SF troops not only in the language, but also with dialects, as well as customs of the country. Each of the Special Forces Groups will also have a language lab for follow-up training.

The next step for the new Green Beret is going to SERE (Survival, Escape, Resistance, and Evasion) School. An SF soldier, or ODA, may be deployed to any location in the world. It may be in the middle of the desert or the side of a mountain; it may range from the extreme heat of the jungle or the frigid cold of subarctic

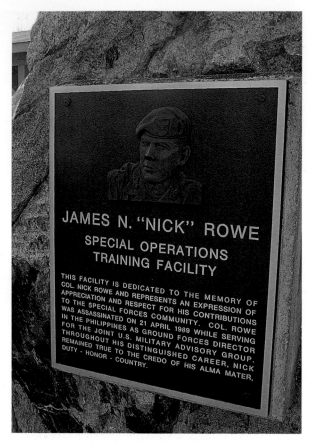

On 8 February 1990, the Rowe Training Facility at Camp MacKall was dedicated in honor of Colonel James N. "Nick" Rowe. Colonel Rowe had survived as a prisoner of war in Vietnam for a period of five years, until he managed to escape from his captors. Colonel Rowe was killed in the Philippines during his tour as senior adviser to that country.

lines; and it is not outside the realm of possibility that he will be captured. The SERE School was developed for these reasons and is mandatory training for all SF soldiers. The school is located at the Colonel Nick Rowe Training Facility, at Camp MacKall. Here, members of Company A, 1st SWTG(A), will impart their survival skills to the students.

The key word for the course is S-U-R-V-I-V-A-L. The students will learn that each of these letters represents a technique. By learning all eight of the skills, they will afford themselves a greater chance of staying alive and returning to base. The eight skills are as follows: S: Size up the situation (the surroundings, your physical condition, equipment); U: Undue haste makes waste; R: Remember where you are; V: Vanquish fear and panic; I: Improvise; V: Value living; A: Act like the natives; and L: Live by your wits (or for the new students, L: Learn basic skills). Put them all together and they spell SURVIVAL, the difference between life and death.

The objective of the course is "to provide students with an understanding of what to expect if captured; explain the Code of Conduct and provide a clear understanding of what is expected of them should they become a prisoner of war (POW); prepare the student to survive in unique and adverse conditions, and to evade the enemy; teach resistance to exploitation by the enemy if captured, and to escape captivity and return home with honor." The SERE course lasts 19 days, ending in an evasion exercise that will expose the SF soldier to increased levels of physical and mental pressure, testing their endurance as well as their resolve. During this course, students will also receive instruction in hand-to-hand combat and sentry take-down techniques. Upon successful completion of the course, the students go through a critique and graduation. At this point the SF soldier will head off to his appropriate group as a new member of an ODA.

regions. Most of the time the team will be working together, and will draw on each other's strengths. There may be times, however, when an SF member could find himself alone, with little or no personal equipment. Due to the very nature of the Special Forces missions, it is very likely he will find himself behind enemy

Warrant Officer Technical Certification Course

The 1st SWTG(A) also teaches the Special Operation Warrant Officer Technical Certification course. The training provides for growth within the SF organization, as it draws from senior Special Forces NCOs. The experienced sergeants, who will have already taken the Army's basic warrant officer program, will receive additional training in special operation command structure, missions, mission preparations, doctrine, SERE, UW classes, isolation, and briefbacks. The training duration is 19 weeks, and culminates with a field training exercise (FTX), Mystic Watchman. Those soldiers graduating from this program are commissioned as warrant officers and go on to serve as the executive officer on an SF ODA.

Advanced Special Forces Skills

Training for the Special Forces soldier never ends. While he continues to hone the skills learned during the Q-course, he will also receive additional training in a variety of techniques to assist him in executing his mission with the greatest probability of success.

Military Free Fall (MFF)

Further airborne infiltration training is available to SF soldiers through the U.S. Army Military Freefall Parachutist School at Ft. Bragg, North Carolina. The mission of the school is to train personnel in the science of HALO (High Altitude Low Opening) military free-fall parachuting, using the Ram-Air Parachute System (RAPS). MFF parachuting enables the theater commander to infiltrate an SF team into an area that would prohibit the use of static-line parachute operations. Special operations missions require rapid and covert infiltration into operational areas.

During week one of this course, the future SF troopers will go through the normal in-processing

High Altitude Low Opening (HALO) and High Altitude High Opening (HAHO) techniques are taught to those SF members who are assigned to a HALO team. Here a member of the 7th Special Forces Group (Airborne) floats down to earth on the Ram-Air Parachute System (RAPS). This jumper is prepared to drop his rucksack, which is suspended by webbing straps. Note the M4A1 carbine tucked along his left side.

and be issued their equipment. At this time they will be assigned to a HALO instructor who will remain with them throughout the four-week training cycle. It is also during week one that they will be matched up with a "jump buddy." Their "buddy" will be approximately the same weight and height, so they will fall at the same rate.

In ground school they will learn about the ram air parachutes, substantially different from the usual T-10B or MCI-1B that they jumped with at Basic Airborne School. The MC-5 ram air parachutes are rectangular shaped as opposed to circular, and are extremely maneuverable. Course students learn about equipment, rigging, and repacking the parachutes. They also learn special jump commands, as well as use of the oxygen systems employed in high altitude jumping.

In case of trouble, the course also teaches emergency procedures involving parachute malfunctions, cutaways, entanglements, and how to recover. These exercises are run over and over until they become second nature to the jumpers. Falling at a rate of over 180 feet per second, you do not have the luxury of thinking about the problem—you must react.

During week one, the candidate spends time in the Military Free Fall Simulator Facility. Completed at Ft. Bragg in 1992 at a cost of $5 million, this 11,000-square-foot facility contains an enclosed vertical wind tunnel, 32 student classrooms, an operator control room, and communications and equipment rooms. "This facility is a marked improvement," says Carol Darby of the Special Warfare School. "Prior to having the facility, the students had to practice [body stabilization] by lying on table tops."

The simulator is approximately 18 feet high and 14 feet in diameter, and it can support two jumpers with equipment up to 375 pounds each. The simulator's fan generates winds up to 132 miles per hour. Suspended in a column of air, the students will learn and practice body-stabilization techniques. The wind tunnel will simulate the effects of free-falling at a speed of approximately 200 feet per second.

After they complete ground week, the students will travel to Yuma Proving Grounds, Arizona. Weeks two through five will find our candidates jumping, jumping, and jumping again, beginning at 10,000 feet with no equipment, and working up to 25,000 feet with full equipment load and oxygen system. The course provides in-the-air instruction, where the student will concentrate on stability, aerial maneuvers and parachute-deployment procedures. Each student will receive a minimum of 16 free fall jumps, which include two day and two night jumps with oxygen and full field equipment.

SCUBA Training

U.S. Army Combat Divers School is in Key West, Florida. At this location, our man will learn to use SCUBA gear to stealthily infiltrate his target area. This training is essential to the SF teams, since they may be asked to infiltrate into denied territory via underwater methods. Unlike U.S. Navy SEALs operations, for the most part Special Forces missions do not take place in the water. The water is merely a means of infiltration and/or transportation to their deployment or objective.

Training will include waterborne operations both day and night. Students will be taught ocean subsurface navigation, deep diving techniques, marine hazards, how to read tides, waves, and currents. They will also be instructed in the proper procedures of submarine lock-in and lock-out, the method of entering and exiting a submerged sub. Training in both open-circuit and closed-circuit equipment will be taught. This is no recreation diving, as depths in training go down to 120 feet under diverse operating conditions.

This training phase will last four weeks. Week one begins with PT, and further physical conditioning to get the trainee prepared for the balance of the class. Week two will find the trooper in the water receiving training to build up his confidence and strengthen his swimming. In week three, students will dive, dive, and then dive some more.

In the final week each student will perform an underwater compass swim. It is not sufficient

Some SF soldiers are trained on SCUBA (Self-contained underwater breathing apparatus) techniques. When necessary for an over-the-horizon insertion, the SF may use LAR-V rebreathers or open circuit systems. This combat swimmer has come ashore to perform a beach recon prior to bringing the balance of the team onto the shore.

to just know how to SCUBA dive; he must be able to execute his mission via underwater ingress. Equipped with a compass board, SCUBA tank, weapon, and rucksack, he will carry out an infiltration to a point on the beach. Final week brings more night dives, a Field Training Exercise, and graduation.

Special Operation Target Interdiction Course (SOTIC)

The SOTIC, as explained by Major Kimm Rowe, commander Company D, 2nd Battalion 1st SWTG(Λ), "trains SF personnel in the technical skills and operational procedures necessary to deliver precision rifle fire from concealed positions to selected targets in support of special operations forces missions." This is also known as sniper training. SOTIC students all volunteer for this training. They must have a rating of expert with their weapon, pass a number of psychological evaluations, and have Secret clearance. SOTIC is a Level 1 category course for Special Forces and Rangers. This means those who graduate from the course are qualified to instruct U.S. troops, train soldiers from foreign nations, and shoot at close proximity to U.S. troops and noncombatants. What that means in simple terms is that a SOTIC sniper can drop an enemy if he is standing right next to you.

The class has a ratio of one SOTIC instructor for every four students, and the students learn the ins and outs of the M24 Sniper Weapon System (SWS), a bolt-action, single-shot rifle chambered in 7.52mm x 51mm; the Leupold Mark IV M3A 10 power rifle scope; XM144 15x-45x spotting scope; and M19/22 binoculars. They will familiarize themselves with the Soviet SVD 7.62mm x 39mm, the Barrett M82A1, 50 caliber, the Stoner SR25, 7.62mm x 51mm and various other U.S. and foreign sniper weapons. They will also receive training in the use of night vision devices, and in the technique and creation of the ghillie suit.

The ghillie suit is a camouflage suit that is used to break up the outline of the sniper. There are a number of options and it often boils down simply to personal preference. The two most common versions, however, are the one-piece, made from a flight suit, and the two-piece BDU version with separate shirt and trousers. The student sews netting onto the clothing, attaches various lengths

SF soldiers may also attend the Special Operations Target Interdiction Course (SOTIC) at Ft. Bragg, North Carolina. SOTIC, better known as sniper training, is the best the U.S. military has to offer. SOTIC is a Level 1 category course for Special Forces and Rangers. Level 1 means, in simple terms, that an SOTIC sniper can drop an enemy if he is standing right next to you.

of burlap to the netting, and then strip by strip shreds the burlap until the outline of the uniform has vanished. A "boonie hat" is often given the same treatment to break up the silhouette of the sniper's head, and then is used for concealment once in position. Vegetation is often added to the burlap for further camouflage. The instructors at the SOTIC favor a mix of 30 percent burlap strips and 70 percent vegetation, which is stuffed into the netting and held in place by rubber bands. One of the SOTIC instructors explains, "By using the local vegetation, the sniper will blend into his surroundings." Students also learn to adjust the foliage in the suit as they move from one position to the next to remain invisible.

During one of the stalking phases, the student-sniper must get to within 200 meters of the spotters. These spotters are SOTIC instructors with ranger finders and binoculars who scan the woodline for the students as they stealthily approach. When the student has reached his position and is confident he has not been sighted, he will fire a blank round. The instructor will call in one of the "walkers" who are out in the brush. They are there to tag the student out if he is spotted. SOTIC instructor, SFC George Simmons, radios to the walker, "Move three feet to your left . . . sniper there." The walker, who knows where the snipers are but does not tell the spotters, responds that he is not within three feet of the sniper who has just fired. Sergeant Simmons then holds up a white card with a number on it. Radio contact is again established with the walker, "Have the student ID the card." The walker responds that the student correctly identifies the number "7." Having moved into position without being sighted, the student is allowed to take a second shot. This time the instructors are looking for telltale signs of a sniper—things like the muzzle blast of the weapon, or the movement of the foliage as the shot is taken. If it's a nada, zip, zero, this student has done well and gets a passing score for the stalk.

During this six-week course, 24 students will be taught the skills of advanced rifle marksmanship, sniper marksmanship, field shooting, field craft, judging distance, observation techniques, camouflage, stalking, counter stalking, and airborne insertion. In the final exercise, the students jump in, move over land, and take a final shot. In a third of the scenarios, they must make a first round hit, or else they don't graduate. Those who do graduate will return to their ODA where they will take up their position as one of two snipers on the team.

Special Operation Training (SOT)

The SOT course was formed back in the late 1970s. SOT trains SOF solders in the tactics, techniques, and procedures required to conduct direct action and unilateral special operations that are of limited scope and duration. SOT also develops the precision marksmanship needed in the MOUT (Military Operations in Urban Terrain) environment. According to Major Rowe, "The real intent for SOT is to train somewhat organic teams together, thus strengthening team cohesion."

Training emphasis is on advanced marksmanship, ballistic and mechanical breaching, limited explosive breaching, building climbing and rappelling, and Close Quarters Battle (CQB)

in various building environments, culminating in a 24-hour FTX.

SFARTAETC

This is the third course carried out by the instructors of Company D, 2nd battalion, 1st SWTG(A).

This rather long abbreviation stands for Special Forces Advance Reconnaissance, Target Analysis, and Exploitation Techniques Course. Although the course is highly classified, the unclassified description states that "SFARTAETC provides the basic entry level training in the tactics, techniques, and procedures needed by personnel being assigned to a theater CinCs in extremis force (CIF).

Special Forces Advance Reconnaissance, Target Analysis, and Exploitation Techniques Course (SFARTAETC). SFARTAETC provides the basic entry-level training in the tactics, techniques, and procedures needed by personnel being assigned to a theater. These skills include precision marksmanship, integrated CQB, and interpretability with other specifically designated forces.

These skills include: precision marksmanship, integrated CQB, and interpretability with other specifically designated forces."

This eight-week course is a counterterrorism (CT) type of CQB usually involving a hostage, POW, or similar situation. Training will also encompass engaging linear targets. Training emphasizes advanced marksmanship, close proximity shooting; ballistic mechanical and explosive breaching techniques for doors, windows, and walls; building-climbing and -rappelling procedures; fast rope techniques; CQB in multi-team and multi-breach points along with multi-story and multi-building environments; and interoperability techniques. Weapons training includes the M4A1 carbine with Aimpoint and tactical light systems, M9 pistol with tactical light, HK MP5, Remington 870 breaching shotgun, ballistic protection, breaching devices, night vision devices, M155 & MK141 flash bangs, fast rope, and climbing equipment.

SFAUC

Special Forces Advanced Urban Combat (SFAUC) was developed by the U.S. Army Special Forces Command in response to the ever-increasing number of urban operations confronting the SF soldier. The driving force behind the program is Major General William Boykin, who had been in charge of the SF Command until March of 2000, when he assumed command of the Special Warfare Center and School.

The general is very familiar with the cost of urban combat on special operations forces, as he was the commander of 1st Special Operations Detachment - Delta in October 1993. It was during this time that Task Force Ranger, the 160th SOAR(A), and Delta Force were engaged in a firefight for their lives in the streets of Mogadishu, Somalia.

General Boykin initiated the SFAUC program in May 1999 with a plan to have every SF soldier trained in the three-week session. Each of the SF groups are responsible to disseminate these techniques and procedures to their ODAs. Major Richard Steiner, Operations Officer, 2nd Battalion, 3rd Special Forces Group (Airborne) explains, "The intent of Special Forces Advanced Urban Combat is to improve Special Forces soldiers' already formidable skills in CQB, especially as it concerns direct action missions, raids and ambushes—and especially as they apply to conducting direct action missions in an urban environment." The world is urbanizing, the population is becoming more and more dense, and SF must be able to operate in that environment. According to Major Steiner, "National Command Authority assumes when they commit Special Operations Forces in general and Special Forces in particular they're getting soldiers that can apply lethal force with a high degree of precision. SFAUC is not necessarily for hostage rescue, rather to pick an enemy out and engage that enemy without a number of unwanted casualties or unwanted collateral damage. SFAUC may be applied in the force protection arena. Where zero U.S. casualties in peacetime or in combat is the goal, then SF must be dominant in CQB tactics. This would include during a DA or even in a SR mission, anywhere in the world. He will have the capability of doing that in a dominating way while still maintaining the precision of U.S. SOF."

SFAUC is operations in urban terrain, involving engaging only hostile or theater enemy forces, sophisticated shooting techniques, identifying the target and engaging, breaching and entering buildings. The SF soldier is trained for every contingency, from bamboo huts to reinforced steel doors—get in and leave the building standing. This is contrary to the Russians' approach: One only has to look at Chechnya to see how they define urban combat—lots of rubble, not very precise.

SFAUC is taught in three phases. Phase I is Combat Marksmanship, advanced shooting skills

As the world urbanizes and the population becomes more dense, the SF soldiers must be able to operate in that environment. SFAUC—Special Forces Advanced Urban Combat—is operations in urban terrain. The skills taught involve engaging only hostile or theater enemy forces, sophisticated shooting techniques, identifying the target and engaging, breaching, and entering buildings. The U.S. Army Special Forces continually hone these skills to ensure they remain the premier special operations fighting force.

with the M4A1 carbine and the M-9 pistol. Targets are engaged from 0 to 50 meters—single targets, multiple targets, from the prone, kneeling, and standing positions. Targets are engaged head-on and laterally and in depth. During this time the soldier will undergo stress firing, 2-1/2 minutes to ID and engage 20–25 targets in various scenarios. He will also face pop-up targets, reactive, and non-reactive targets, from 3–25 meters. He will fire and reload using his primary weapon (M4A1) and secondary weapon (M-9).

Phase II covers Breaching/CQB. Mechanical breaching involves the use of sledge hammers, battering rams, crowbars, and glass and bolt cutters.

Ballistic breaching is using a shotgun with a variety of ammunition, such as #9 bird shot and "shock locks" and other specialty ammo to defeat a door, primarily the locking mechanism. Explosive breaching covers a diverse selection of explosives and techniques—flex linear charge, det-cord, C-4. A favorite is the silhouette charge—a cardboard silhouette with one to three wraps of det-cord around the perimeter, with a charge to the center does a good job of cutting through a door. Replace the det-cord with the proper amount of C-4 and the silhouette will now blow out a substantial passageway through a cinder block wall. Assorted initiators are also taught for instant detonation.

Phase III is CQB. During this phase the SF will be trained in and practice single-man, two-man, and four-man entry into a room, engaging targets, and collapsing on their sector. They will learn how to "stack," which is lining up for dynamic entry into a room or building. The SF soldiers will conduct a breach, enter the building, clear the room, secure the structure; if on a DA mission, they will recover personnel or equipment, or destroy the target, and clear the structure.

While each mission will vary, the standard deployment for SF CQB is the four-man entry team. From the time the team members initiate the breach, enter the room, collapse and secure their sector, finally clearing the room, it will take an average of four seconds.

The SF primary weapon for SFAUC training is the M-4 carbine. Choice of scopes range from standard iron sight, ACOG 4x scope, Aimpoint with red dot, or ACOG Reflex sight—the latter two are used with both eyes open. Additionally the M-4 carbine may be fitted with a white light that has a pressure on/off switch. It may be used for securing an individual, or searching a room once secure. The SFAUC troops may choose a more stealthy approach and go in with weapons suppressed. Major Steiner says, "Since the 5.56mm round is supersonic, you will hear the bang. What the suppressor does for you is buy you some time while the bad guys are trying to figure out, 'what was that?' 'Where did it come from?' By the time they figure out what is going on, you should be in dominance of the situation." Suppressors will also keep the muzzle blast to a minimum, assisting the entry team in situation awareness.

Weapons are not the only edge the SFAUC Green Beret has in his kit. Currently the SF ODAs are looking at a new headgear for CQB, a combination Kevlar and communications helmet. In the meantime, they will continue to train with the current Kevlars. During the three-week session, with an average of 36 students, the SFAUC course will expend more than 75,000 rounds of 5.56mm ball, 75,000 rounds of 9mm ball, 15,000 rounds of simmunitions (simulated munitions, using a plastic bullet), and hundreds of 12 gauge assorted loads.

There is a reason for the amount of ammunition used. Some would call it "muscle-memory," in which the body automatically brings the weapon up to the ready. Others called it automatic response. Whatever term you choose, SFAUC trains the SF soldier in the fundamentals of sight alignment and trigger control. Once you can reflexively apply those two skills, you will get hits, whether you are standing on the corner, sitting in a HUMMV, or jogging down the street. The SF soldier is taught to neutralize the hostile until he is no longer a threat.

SFAUC is about engaging hostiles in a DA or SR mission. This is not intended to replace the training for hostage rescue. The techniques and procedures taught in this course will aid the SF soldier as he takes down a radar installation or command post, recovers equipment, or deals with guards. SF takes weapons skills so seriously that there are four "shooting houses" on Ft. Bragg alone. Major Tom McCollum, SF Command, relates, "These guys are just about artists at their profession. The training is repetitive, and you build on those skills. Then you begin to use your imagination, to think outside of the box: What if . . . ? Suppose we do this . . . ? Then you build in the contingencies for the what-ifs."

All of the training, and the acclimation of that training, is the reason the SF soldiers are in constant demand around the globe. Their advanced training is what makes them the Quiet Professionals within the U.S. military, and provides the expertise that makes the Special Forces soldiers the most lethal warriors on earth.

7 Equipment and Techniques

Special Forces soldiers are schooled in unconventional techniques and procedures that will prove beneficial to their missions. The communications sergeant is capable of rigging up a radio antenna with some branches, 550 cord and Meal Ready to Eat (MRE) spoons. The engineer sergeant, with items from under the kitchen sink, can construct an explosive devise to take out a target, while the weapons sergeant is able to assemble an assortment of lethal weapons, from slingshots to shotguns. SF soldiers are trained to be effective with whatever is at hand. But in real-world situations, where they are almost always vastly outnumbered, these men are equipped with the best weapons and technology available to fulfill their missions.

Weapons

Special Forces soldiers are familiar with and expert in numerous types of weapons systems, U.S. and foreign, new and old, allied and enemy. They must know how to operate a World War II German MG34 machine gun being used in a Third World country, or the latest Mark 19, 40mm Grenade Machine Gun, in use with Coalition Forces. They are masters of small arms, such as revolvers, semi-automatic pistols, rifles, and submachine guns. Use of crew-served weapons, like the 60mm and 81mm mortar, and recoilless rifles is a common task for the SF troopers. Where is the best place to position a .30 caliber or .50 caliber machine gun? The SF will instruct in the placement, fire lanes, and interlocking fields of fire to maximize these lethal instruments. Engaging an enemy tank or bunker? The Operational

Detachment-Alpha (ODA) will survey which system will best do the job—e.g., the AT-4, Carl Gustov, or M-72 LAW. Whether engaging personnel, tanks, helicopters, buildings, or aircraft, the Special Forces soldiers are the best trained fighters in the world to accomplish this mission.

To cover all of the weapons systems in use by the Special Forces Groups would require volumes.

The M9 9mm Berretta pistol was adopted by the Department of Defense to standardize the 9mm round for U.S. and NATO forces. The M9 is the standard issue pistol for all U.S. military troops including the Special Forces. While it is an acceptable weapon, there are many within the special operations community who still favor the .45 caliber round.

Consequently, we will address those weapons organic to the ODA, the primary firearms intrinsic to the team.

SOPMOD M4A1

All Special Forces soldiers are currently issued the Special Operations Peculiar Modification (SOPMOD) M4A1 Carbine. The M4A1 from Colt Arms of Connecticut is a smaller, compact version of the full-sized M16A2 rifle. This weapon was designed specifically for the U.S. Special Operations Forces. The M4A1 is designed for speed of action and light weight. The barrel has been redesigned to a shortened 14.5 inches, which reduces the weight while maintaining the gun's effectiveness for quick-handling field operations. The retractable butt stock has intermediate stops allowing versatility in Close Quarters Battle (CQB) without compromising shooting capabilities.

The M4A1 has a rifling twist of 1 in 7 inches, making it compatible with the full range of 5.56mm ammunitions. Its sighting system contains dual apertures, one for 0–200 meters and a smaller opening for targets at 500–600 meters. Selective fire controls for the M4A1 have eliminated the three-round burst, replacing it with safe semi-automatic and full automatic fire.

The SOPMOD Accessory Kit allows the SF soldier to modify the weapon per mission parameters. Using the Rail Interface System (RIS), numerous components may be secured to the weapon. The kit includes a 4x32mm Trijicon Day Optical Scope, allowing the soldiers to judge range and deliver more accurate fire out to 300 meters; Trijicon Reflex sight, designed for close-in engagement; and Infrared Target Pointer/Illuminator/Aiming Laser AN/PEQ-2 (for use with night vision devices), which places a red aiming dot on the target—very useful in building and CQB. Additionally, the kit includes Visible Light, a high-intensity flashlight mounted on the rail system; backup iron sight (since the carrying handle of the M4A1 can be removed, this backup sight can be employed in the absence of the handle); and a forward hand grip, which helps in stabilization of the weapon and keeps the user's hands away from the hand guards and barrel, which tend to heat up in combat. Finally, the kit includes a sound suppressor, which significantly reduces the noise and muzzle blast.

The primary weapon for the Special Forces soldier is the Colt M4A1 Carbine. This shortened version of the M16A2 rifle features a collapsible stock, a flat top upper receiver with an accessory rail, and a detachable handle and aperture sight assembly. The M4A1 fire selector has three settings: safe, full automatic, or single shot. The M4A1 shown here has been modified with the Special Operations Peculiar Modification (SOPMOD) accessory kit. A special Rail Interface System (RIS) allows the attachment of numerous aiming devices and accessories depending on the mission. This M4A1 has been modified with a Trijicon ACOG (Advanced Combat Optical Gun-sight) 4x32 scope; on the handgrip is a AN/PEQ-2 Infrared Target Pointer/Illuminator/Aiming Device. The PEQ-2 emits a laser beam for precise aiming of the weapon. It may also be used for lasing targets for the delivery of smart bombs. Finally, attached to the barrel is a Quick Attach/Detach Sound Suppressor. With the suppressor attached the muzzle, blast, flash, and sound are significantly reduced.

The M203 grenade launcher is a lightweight, single-shot breech loaded 40mm weapon specifically designed for placement beneath the barrel of the M4A1 Carbine. With a quick- release mechanism, the addition of the M203 to M4A1 carbine creates the versatility of a weapon system capable of firing both 5.56mm ammunition as well as an expansive range of 40mm high explosive and special purpose munitions.

Colt M203

The M203 grenade launcher is a lightweight (three-pound), single-shot, breech-loaded 40mm weapon specifically designed for placement beneath the barrel of the M16A1 and M16A2 rifles and M4A1/M16A2 carbines. Attached with a quick-release mechanism, the M203 creates the versatility of a weapon system capable of firing both 5.56mm ammunition as well as an expansive range of 40mm high explosive and special purpose munitions.

The most commonly utilized M203 ammunition is the M406 antipersonnel round. This grenade has a deadly radius of five meters. Another option is the M433 multi-purpose grenade, which in addition to the fragmentation effects is capable of penetrating steel armor plate up to two inches thick. Other types of ordnance available are buckshot, tear gas, and various signal rounds.

The receiver of the M203 is manufactured of high-strength forged aluminum alloy. This provides extreme ruggedness, while keeping weight to a minimum. A complete self-cocking firing mechanism, including striker, trigger, and positive safety lever, is included in the receiver. This will allow the M203 to be operated as an independent weapon, even though attached to the M16A1 or M16A2 rifle or M4A1/M16A2 carbine. The barrel is also made of high-strength aluminum alloy, which has been shortened from 12 to 9 inches, allowing improved balance and handling. It slides forward in the receiver to accept a round of ammunition, then slides backward to automatically lock in the closed position, ready to fire.

Special Operations Forces depend on rapid deployment, mobility, and increased firepower. Where the emphasis of a small unit, such as the SF, is placed on "get in and get out" fast, the M203 lends added firepower to the already-proven and outstanding family of M16 weapons.

M9 Beretta

Since 1985, the M9 has seen service as the standard issue side arm for U.S. troops, both conventional and special, in Operation Urgent Fury in Grenada, Operation Desert Shield/Storm in Kuwait, Operation Restore Hope in Somalia, and with IFOR in Bosnia and KFOR in Kosovo. Along with the standardization of the 9mm round, the M9 brought the armed forces a larger-capacity magazine. The M9 holds 15 rounds, compared to the Colt 1911's seven or eight rounds. Although the 9mm ammunition was lighter and smaller, it was viewed as ade-

The M240B replaces the M-60 machine gun in the ODAs (Operational Detachment-Alpha). The highly reliable 7.62mm machine gun delivers more energy to the target than the smaller caliber M249 Squad Assault Weapon (SAW) in use with the Rangers and other Army troops.

ment Company. The smooth cylindrical suppresser is manufactured of anodized aluminum with a steel attachment system. Weighing a scant 6 ounces, it can be replaced or removed in three seconds. Carrying over the Vietnam-era name, the suppressor was dubbed the "Hush-Puppy."

M-240 Medium Machine Gun

After extensive operational testing, the U.S. Army selected the M240B medium machine gun as a replacement for the M60 family of machine guns. Manufactured by Fabrique Nationale, the 24.2 pound M240B medium machine gun is a gas-operated, air-cooled, linked-belt-fed weapon that fires the 7.62 x 51 mm round. The weapon fires from an open bolt position with a maximum effective range of 1,100 meters. The rate of fire is adjustable from 750 to 1400 rounds per minute through an adjustable gas regulator. It features a folding bipod that attaches to the receiver, a quick-change barrel assembly, a feed cover and bolt assembly enabling closure of the cover regardless of bolt position, a plastic butt stock and an integral optical sight rail. While it possesses many of the same characteristics as the older M60, the durability of the M240 system results in superior reliability and maintainability.

M249 Squad Automatic Weapon (SAW)

Fielded in the mid-1980s, the M249 SAW is an individually portable, air-cooled, belt-fed, gas-operated light machine gun. A unique feature of the SAW is the number of alternate ammunition feeds. The standard ammunition load is 200 rounds of 5.56mm ammunitions in disintegrating belts. These rounds are fed from a 200-round plastic ammunition box through the side of the weapon. The normal link ammunition for the SAW is four rounds of M855 ball ammunitions followed by one round of M85 tracer. Additionally, it can use standard 20- and 30-round M16 magazines, which

quate for line troops. This trade-off also allowed the troops to engage more rounds in a fire fight before having to reload. The original M9 was viewed with some apprehension among operators in the Special Operations community because +P ammunition reportedly caused stress fractures of the weapon's slides. Beretta addressed this problem and today's M9 has an average life of 72,250 rounds.

The slide is open for nearly the entire length of the barrel. This facilitates the ejection of spent shells and virtually eliminates stoppages. The open slide configuration also provide a means for the pistol to be loaded manually. As with all weapons in use with Special Operation Forces, the operators are always trying to get that extra "edge." One of the most likely features to be added to the M9 was a sound suppressor. For such a device the military turned to Knight Arma-

M249 SAW is an individually portable, air-cooled, belt-fed, gas-operated light machine gun. The standard load is 200 rounds of 5.56mm ammunitions in disintegrating belts. These rounds are fed from a 200-round plastic ammunition box through the side of the weapon. Additionally, the SAW can utilize standard 20- and 30-round M4A1/M16 magazines, which are inserted in a magazine well in the bottom of the SAW. Using the same 5.56mm ammunition as the M4A1, it allows the ODA to carry common ammunition loads. The M249 is capable of engaging targets out to 800 meters.

The weapon of choice for the Special Forces sniper is the M24 SWS, or Sniper Weapon System. Based on a Remington 700 action, it is equipped with a Leupold Mark IV 10 power fixed scope referred to as the "Ma-3 Alpha." The M24 SWS is a bolt-action rifle capable of engaging a target at well over 500 meters.

are inserted in a magazine well in the bottom of the SAW. Since the SAW uses the same 5.56mm ammunition as the M4A1, it allows the ODA to carry common ammunition loads. The M249 is capable of engaging targets out to 800 meters.

M24 Sniper Weapon System (SWS)

The current issue sniper rifle for the Special Forces is the M24 SWS, two per ODA. The M24 is based on the Remington 700 series long action. This action accommodates chambering for either the 7.62x51mm or .300 Winchester Magnum round. The rifle is a bolt-action six-shot repeating rifle (one round in the chamber and five additional rounds in the magazine). It is issued with the Leupold Mark IV 10 power M3A scope, commonly referred to as the "Ma-3-Alpha." The sniper

may also make use of the weapon's iron sights. Attached to the scope is the M24/EMA ARD (Anti-Reflection Device). Less than three inches long, this honeycomb of tubes cuts down the glare of the scope. The M24 SWS does come with a Harris bipod; however, most of the time the bipod remains in the deployment case. The rifle weighs 12.1 pounds without the scope and has an overall length of 43 inches, with a free-floating barrel of 24 inches. The stock is composite Kevlar, graphite, and fiberglass with an aluminum-bedding block. The stock has an adjustable butt plate to accommodate the length of pull.

Heavy Sniper Rifle

When the mission calls for a Hard Target Interdiction (HTI) at very long range, e.g., over 1,000 meters, the SF will turn to the big guns. HTI would be taking out such targets as an airplane, helicopter, or vehicle. Currently, the SF has the M82A1 in their inventories. It is a one-man portable, semi-automatic rifle with a magazine

When hard targets must be engaged over 1,000 meters away, the SF will turn to the Barrett M82A1 semi-automatic .50 caliber rifle. Here a member of the 5th Special Forces Group (Airborne) is inundated with the desert sand as he sends rounds down range. The M82A1 currently in the SF armory will soon be augmented with the M107 bolt-action, magazine-feed .50 caliber rifle.

Mark 19, 40mm Grenade Machine Gun is a self-powered, air-cooled, belt-fed, blow-back operated weapon. The MK19 is designed to deliver accurate, intense, and decisive firepower against enemy personnel and lightly armored vehicles.

holding up to 10 rounds of .50 caliber Browning machine gun (BMG) ammunition. These are group weapons and are drawn out per mission requirements. Now that the SF soldiers are in the new millennium, USASOC will add a new .50 caliber weapon to their Table of Organization and Equipment (T.O.& E.). Each ODA will now be issued one Barrett M107 .50 caliber rifle. The M107 weighs 23 pounds, with a length of 45 inches. It can be reduced in size by further take-down of the weapon, allowing for more covert transport. Using a bullpup design, it is a bolt-action system with a removable five-round magazine, and is chambered for all NATO .50 caliber BMG cartridges. Other features include a quick-detachable bipod with spiked feet, iron sights, and an M1913 (Picatinny) optical rail to accommodate various sighting and aiming devices. The addition of the M107 to the T.O.&E. will give the Special Forces more punch, readily accessible to the A-teams.

Vehicles

GMV (Ground Mobility Vehicle)

The GMV has its origins in Desert Storm. During the Gulf War, the Special Forces modified HUMMVs for extended desert missions, dubbing them DUMMV (pronounced "Dum-Vee"). The modifications included a heavier suspension, more powerful engine, and an open bed and back for storage of water and fuel and other mission-essential item. The GMV has a cupola on top, similar to that used for mounting a tow system. It is used for mounting various weapons systems, e.g., M2, .50 caliber

The Ground Mobility Vehicle, or GMV, had its origins in Desert Storm. During the Gulf War, the Special Forces modified HUMMVs for extended desert missions, dubbing them DUMMVs, pronounced "Dum-Vee." The modifications included a heavier suspension, more powerful engine, and an open bed and back for storage of water and fuel and other mission-essential items. The GMV has a cupola on top, similar to that used for mounting a TOW missile system. It is used for mounting various weapons systems, e.g., the M2 .50 caliber machine gun and the Mark 19, 40mm Grenade Machine Gun.

The F470 Zodiac Inflatable Boat is the mainstay of water-borne operations with Special Forces. Extremely versatile, it can be launched from submarines and other boats. It can be air dropped via parachute or other deployment methods from an assortment of fixed- and rotary-wing aircraft. When using the outboard motor, the Zodiac is fast and quiet.

machine gun and the Mark 19, 40mm grenade machine gun.

Used by the SF Mounted Teams, the basic make-up is four GMV per team, with a crew of three men per vehicle. The GMV greatly enhances the capability of the mounted ODAs, extending their mission endurance and flexibility.

According the Colonel Gary Jones, Commander 3rd SFG(a), Mounted Team soldiers attend special schools, such as the Rod Hall

Advanced Military Off-Road driver training in the desert of Nevada. Here they are taught how to drive the GMV safely and effectively in on-road and off-road environments. The Special Forces soldiers learn techniques such as brake modulation, which allows them to work the ups and downs of the harsh environment and navigate over rocky, uneven terrain. The soldiers also learn how to maintain the vehicle and make necessary repairs in the field.

Zodiac Rafts

The F470 Zodiac Inflatable Boat is the mainstay of water-borne operations with Special Forces. Extremely versatile, it can be launched from submarines and other boats. It can be air dropped via parachute or other deployable methods from an assortment of fixed- and rotary-wing aircraft. When using the outboard

Wearing PVS7 Night Vision Goggles and carrying M4A1s, two members of the 3rd Special Forces Group (Airborne) infiltrate under the cover of darkness. The Klepper Arius 2 Military Canoe, more commonly referred to as a sea kayak, features speed and stealth. The canoe gives the lowest signature of all the surface vessels in use by U.S. Special Operations Forces.

motor, the Zodiac is fast and quiet. Each fuel bladder will allow the craft approximately one hour of operation with an average load of six men and equipment. The low profile and the fabric provide little or no radar signature to be detected by hostile forces. An interesting cache method that can be deployed in a team insertion is to totally submerge the Zodiac, caching the boat, outboard, and other equipment. Upon mission completion, the team will return to position, locate the boat and, using special compressed air tanks, reinflate it, power up the outboard, and exfil the area.

Klepper Arius 2 Military Canoe

The Klepper is more commonly referred to as a sea kayak. It possesses many of the Zodiac's advantages, except for air droppability and motor operations. The sea kayak features speed and stealth. Using the paddles, a crew of two can travel extended distances in a relatively short time. The canoe gives the lowest signature of all the surface vessels in use by U.S. Special Operations Forces. The two SF soldiers sit just below sea level with only their upper torsos elevated above the clandestine craft. Their Load Bearing Equipment and mission-essential equipment are placed in storage positions within the craft.

Snow Terrain Vehicle

For operations in snow-covered mountains, the Special Forces teams employ a snow terrain vehicle, "mil-speak" for snowmobiles. Currently in the inventory of the 10th SFG(A) are Polaris Model 600, wide track, 500cc machines. Each man on the ODA will have his own snowmobile, allowing the team to run split-team operations and provide backup transportation of team members should one of the snowmobiles break down or become disabled in combat. The SF soldiers load up the snowmobiles with kit gear, snowshoes, snow shovel, tent, and food. The M4A1 weapons are placed in an M1950 rifle case mounted on the side of the unit. Additionally, each member will carry a minimum of three five-gallon cans of fuel. One of the techniques employed by the 18Ds is placing IV bags in an

The Army calls it a Snow Terrain Vehicle, more commonly known as a snowmobile. This Polaris Model 600 is currently in use with the 10th SFG(A). Each man on the ODA has his own snowmobile, which he will load up with his kit gear, snowshoes, snow shovel, tent, and food. The M4A1 weapons are placed in an M1950 rifle case mounted on the side of the unit.

ammo can under the cowling next to the engine. In the event one must be used, it is not only not frozen, but warm so as not to lower the patient's body temperature when administered. Team members have also found this procedure useful for warming their Meals Ready to Eat (MREs). In addition to the snowmobiles, the teams also employ sleds called "Pulks" to carry their rucksacks and other mission-essential equipment.

Global Positioning System (GPS)

While all Special Forces soldiers are trained in land navigation using the standard issue Lensetic Compass, sometimes the A-team must have pinpoint accuracy, as when conducting an SR mission through the desert, or across the frozen tundra, in enemy territory, in the middle of the night. They will need to know the position of an enemy division, a radar station, or perhaps a SCUD when reporting in to headquarters. For such instances they will use a device known as a Global Positioning System or GPS.

The GPS is a collection of satellites that orbit the earth twice a day. During this orbiting they transmit precise time, latitude, longitude, and altitude information. Using a GPS receiver, special operations forces can ascertain their exact location anywhere on the earth. It is the same technology used by certain civilian automobile navigation services.

GPS was developed by the U.S. Department of Defense (DOD) in the early 1970s to provide a continuous, worldwide positioning and navigational system for U.S. military forces around the globe. The complete constellation, as it is called, consists of 24 satellites orbiting approximately 12,000 miles above the earth. These 22 active and two reserve or backup satellites provide data 24 hours a day for 2D and 3D positioning anywhere on the planet. Each satellite constantly broadcasts precise time and location data. Troops using a GPS receiver receive these signals.

Members of the 5th Special Forces Group (Airborne) call in the position of their Mission Support Site. Using the Rockwell "Plugger" GPS unit, they can convey their exact position to higher headquarters.

By measuring the time interval between the transmission and the receiving of the satellite signal, the GPS receiver calculates the distance between the users and each satellite. Using the distance measurements of at least three satellites in an algorithm computation, the GPS receiver provides the precise location. A special encryption signal is used in the military's Precise Positioning Service. A second signal called Standard Positioning Service is available for civilian and commercial use.

The Special Forces ODAs are issued the Rockwell "Plugger" or PSN-11. The precise name for the unit is PLGR+96 (Precise Lightweight GPS Receiver). The PLGR96 is the most advanced version of the U.S. DOD hand-held GPS unit. It serves the increasingly demanding requirements of the SF soldiers, as well as all the U.S. Special Operations Forces.

Secure (Y-code) Differential GPS allows the user to accept differential correction without zeroing the unit. Differential accuracy can be less than one meter. Other features of the "Plugger" include Wide Area GPS Enhancement for autonomous positioning accuracy to 4 meters CEP, jammer direction finding, targeting interface with laser range-finder, remote display terminal capability, and advanced user interface features.

Weighing in at a mere 2.7 pounds (with batteries installed) the GPS unit is easily stowed in the cavernous rucksack carried by the ODAs. In addition to hand-held operation, the PLGR+96 unit can be installed in various vehicles and airborne platforms.

For missions requiring underwater infiltration, there is the MUGR, Miniature Underwater Global Positioning System Receiver. This small device weighs 1.2 pounds and provides the team with position and navigational information needed for infil/exfil, fire support, Special Reconnaissance, and target location. Once the unit acquires the satellite fix, the waterproof MUGR can be taken to a depth of 33 feet. Alternately, the unit may work underwater employing the optional floating antenna.

SOFLAM

Special Operations Forces - Laser Acquisition Marker (SOFLAM). Special Forces soldiers would use this equipment in a direct action mission for the direction of terminal guided ordnance. This technique is referred to as "lasing the target." When it absolutely, positively has to be destroyed, you put an SF team on the ground and a fast mover with a smart bomb in the air; results—one smoking bomb crater. This newly issued laser marking

Communications is the lifeline of the SF team. Here a member of the 10th Special Forces Group (Airborne) uses the AN/PSC-5 (V) "Shadowfire" by Raytheon.

device is lighter and more compact than the current laser marker in service with the U.S. military. It can be used in daylight, or with the attached night vision optics it can be employed at night.

Radios

Communications is the lifeline of the SF team. For long-range communications, the Special Forces use the AN/PSC-5 (V) "Shadowfire" by Raytheon, issued two per ODA. The PSC-5 is a multi-band, multi-mission communication terminal with capability for UHF/VHF (Ultra High Frequency/Very High Frequency) Manpack LOS

Another useful communication device is the PRC-137. This ultra-lightweight HF radio is unique to Special Operations Forces. Using a small keyboard, the SF soldier will type in the message to be sent; it is then down-loaded into the radio. He then may continue on his mission. When the base station comes online, an automatic link will be established with the PRC-137 and the message will be up-loaded.

(Line-Of-Sight) and satellite communications (SATCOM). For satellite use, the set provides both TDMA (Time Division Multiple Access) and DAMA (Demand Assigned Multiple Access). This device supports the DOD requirement for a lightweight, secure, network-capable, multi-band, multi-mission, anti-jam, voice/imagery/data communication capability in a single package. The Shadowfire weighs 11.7 pounds without the battery, 8 pounds heavier with it.

For tactical intra-team communications, Multi-band Inter/Intra Team radios provide the SF teams with the ability to communicate on user-selected frequencies from 30 to 512 MHz using a single hand-held unit. The radios have power up to 5 watts in VHF/FM, VHF/AM, UHF/AM, UHF/FM(LOS) for ground-to-ground and air-to-ground connectivity. Weighing only 31 ounces, the radios come in two versions, immersible to six feet and 66 feet. The units have embedded COMSEC (Communications Security) for full digital voice and data operations. The MI/IT radio will replace the current AN/PRC-126, AN/PRC-68, Saber I/II/III, and MX-300 Series.

Rappelling

This old mountaineering technique has served SF troops since the first Special Forces soldiers operated in the mountains of Bavaria, near Bad Tolz, Germany. Whether working in a mountainous terrain, or in an urban environment, rappelling is a valuable skill. Often, traversing a steep hill carrying an 80- to 100-pound rucksack, it is the best way down the contour.

SF teams will train in this procedure with full combat gear, as well as rappelling with a casualty. Attaching to a regular military assault line through carabiners, or a specially designed rappelling device (known as a "Figure 8"), the team will negotiate down the side of a mountain like a mountain goat, or the side of a building as rapidly as Spiderman.

This member of the 7th Special Forces Group (Airborne) is suited up for a High Altitude Low Opening (HALO) parachute jump. HALO is one of the means by which SF teams can be inserted into denied or hostile territory. The jumpers are capable of exiting an aircraft at 25,000 feet using oxygen. They will then free fall to a designated altitude where they will open their RAPS and then form up together. This jumper has his rucksack strapped in front and his M4A1 attached to his left side, ready to go.

FRIES

The Fast Rope Insertion/Extraction System is the way to insert your assault force on the ground in seconds. This system begins with small woven ropes made of wool, which are then braided into a larger rope. The rope is rolled into a deployment bag and the end secured to a helicopter. Depending on the model of chopper, it can be just outside on the hoist mechanism of the side door or attached to a bracket off the back ramp. Once over the insertion point the rope is deployed and even as it is hitting the ground the ODA members are jumping onto the woolen line and sliding down, as easily as a fireman goes down a pole. Once the team is safely on the ground the flight engineer or gunner, depending on the type of helicopter, will pull the safety pin and the rope will fall to the ground. Such a system is extremely useful in the rapid deployment of Special Forces personnel. An entire ODA can be inserted within 12–15 seconds. FRIES is the most accepted way of getting a force onto the ground expeditiously. Unlike rappelling, once the trooper hits the ground, he is "free" of the rope and can begin his mission.

The second part of FRIES is the extraction method. Although both insertion and extraction systems were originally referred to as SPIES, or Special Procedure, Insertion & Extraction System, the Army has combined both methods into one term. While fast-roping gets you down quickly, there are times when you have to extract just as fast. The problem is, there is no Landing Zone for the Blackhawk of the 160th SOAR to land, and the "bad guys" are closing in on your position. This technique is similar to the McGuire and STABO rigs developed during the Vietnam War. Both used multiple ropes, which often resulted in the troops colliding with one another; the latter at least let the user fire his weapon while on the ride up. The techniques that served the Special Forces troops of the 1960s have been refined to the new FRIES method.

Fast Rope Insertion/Extraction System or FRIES is the fastest method of inserting Special Forces soldiers. An entire ODA can be inserted within 12–15 seconds. Once over the insertion point the rope is deployed and even as it is hitting the ground the ODA members are jumping onto the woolen line and sliding down, as easily as a fireman goes down a pole. Extremely useful in the rapid deployment of Special Forces personnel, FRIES is the most accepted way of getting a force onto the ground expeditiously. Unlike rappelling, once the trooper hits the ground, he is free of the rope and can begin his mission.

The second part of FRIES is the extraction method. Originally referred to as SPIES, or Special Procedure, Insertion & Extraction System, the system was changed by the Army to combine both methods. While fast-roping gets you down quickly, there are times when you have to extract just as fast. A single rope is lowered from the hovering helicopter. Wearing a special harness, the SF member or team attaches to the rope via snap links. Once the men are secure to the line, the helicopter will whisk the team out of harm's way. *Defense Visual Information Center Photo*

To extract with FRIES, a single rope is lowered from the hovering helicopter. Attached to this rope are rings, woven and secured into the rope at approximately five-foot intervals. There can be as many as eight rings on the rope. The SF soldiers, wearing special harnesses similar to a parachute harness, attach themselves to the rope via the rings. This is accomplished by clipping in a snap link that at the top of the harness. Once all team members are secured, a signal is given and the soldiers are extracted out of harm's way. This method allows the team members to maintain covering fire from their weapons as they extract. Once the SF soldiers have been whisked out of enemy range, and an LZ can be located, the helicopter pilot will bring the troops to ground again.

At this time they will disconnect from the rope and board the chopper to leave the area.

Rubber Duck

A "rubber duck" is the term SOF troops use to describe a mission involving deployment of a Zodiac raft. In a Soft Duck, a fully inflated Zodiac raft is deployed from the rear cargo ramp of a "NightStalker" MH-47 Chinook, or an AFSOC MH-53 Pave Low. The raft is slid out the back of the helicopter and the ODA follows right behind. Once in the water, the team jumps in, fires up the outboard engine, and heads out on its mission. An alternate to this is the Hard Duck, which involves a craft with a metal bottom delivered in the same manner as the Soft Duck. The Zodiac may also be

Members of the 3rd Special Forces Group (Airborne) perform a Rubber Duck operation from an MH-47E. Immediately after the Zodiac raft has cleared the ramp, the SF team will follow it out. Swimming to the raft, they will then load in and continue their insertion to their target area.

deployed via parachute, as would be the case when delivered via AFSOC assets such as a Combat Talon or Combat Shadow. Moments after the loadmaster releases the package, the SF troops will shuffle to the end of the ramp and parachute in after it. An additional method is the Double Duck, where two Zodiacs, fully inflated, are stacked and deployed via parachute together, again via the Hercules aircraft.

Delta Queen

While the Rubber Duck is used for inserting a SF team, the Delta Queen is a method for retrieval and extraction of the team. Upon mission completion the team will return to the Zodiac, and go "feet wet" into the water, whether an ocean, a lake, or river. The team will meet up with an MH-47E Chinook of the 160th Special Operation Air Regiment (Airborne). The pilot will bring his aircraft to a hover, then bring the heli-copter down, closer and closer to the water's surface. He will continue his descent until the rotary-wing craft actually rests on the water.

With the rear cargo ramp lowered, the MH-47E will begin to take on water. Wave after wave begins to cascade over the ramp and soon the flight engineers are standing in water over the tops of their boots. As the Zodiac begins to line up with the rear of the chopper, the crew member holds a red-filtered light to signal the team. The exfiltrating team guns the engine, ducks their heads, and aims for the ramp and the now-flooded fuselage. With a splash and a thud, the team is aboard and already the ramp begins to raise slightly. The pilot raises the behemoth aircraft from the surface, creating what looks like a small version of Niagara Falls as the water pours from the rear of the heli-copter. The extraction complete, the NightStalkers and the Special Forces team or return to base.

"Mission complete. Request Exfil." Called a Delta Queen, the Night Stalker pilot of this MH-47E Chinook will set the large helicopter down so the aircraft is literally taking on water. Guided by members of the flight crew signaling with a flashlight, the SF ODA will then pilot the Zodiac up the ramp and into the fuselage. Once secure, the pilot will lift off and return to base.

8

Special Forces in the 21st Century

When the Special Forces was formed in 1952, the biggest threat to world peace and democracy was from the Soviet Union. The A-teams of the 1950s practiced for Unconventional Warfare (UW) against the Russian "Bear" and made preparations to conduct guerrilla activities in World War III. With the collapse of the Soviet Union, there is a new perspective on warfare. The predication of World War III with masses of Soviet T-80 tanks rolling

Around the world, around the clock. Members of the U.S. Army Special Forces stand poised to defend freedom on a moment's notice. From the frigid Arctic winds to the humid, insect- and snake-infested jungles, the men of the Green Beret carry on in the tradition of their predecessors to defend liberty at all costs.

As the U.S. Army Special Operations Command advances further into the 21st century, the dynamic world of today will find the Special Forces soldier in the position of warrior, diplomat, and commando. Once shunned by conventional troops and commanders, the Special Forces today are in constant demand by U.S. ambassadors and theater CinCs.

Whether preparing for all-out war or OOTW due to the regional instability around the world, they stand poised, mission capable to deploy, on a moment's notice, a threat-adaptive force. During the Cold War the U.S. deterrent to a nuclear holocaust was the Strategic Triad: Inter-Continental Ballistic Missiles in silos, Strategic Air Command bombers flying around the globe, and submarines on patrol. The Special Forces of the 21st Century comprise a new "Triad" for democracy: the Operational Detachment-Alphas (ODAs), the regional orientation of the teams, and the latest specialized equipment.

The Special Forces soldier of the 1950s and 1960s has evolved from a guerrilla/counter-guerrilla fighter to the consummate paragon of special operations. In today's dynamic world the Special Forces soldier is warrior, diplomat, and commando. Once shunned by conventional troops and commanders, the Special Forces today are in constant demand by U.S. Ambassadors and theater CinCs. The ODAs of this century possess strategic agility, ubiquitous presence, state-of-the-art equipment, and the latest intelligence for information dominance.

Strategic agility is the Special Forces' capability to meet the contingency needs of the regionally engaged CinC and Special Operations Command with forces based Outside of Continental United States (OCONUS) and forward-based forces.

Ubiquitous presence is evident in the forward deployed teams, e.g., Europe, Korea, and the Caribbean. In addition to these teams, there are regionally assigned SF Groups to support various engagement plans of the theater CinCs. This regional deployment creates a cultural exchange, establishes credibility, and builds trust and relationships between the SF soldiers and host nation forces. These Foreign Internal Defense (FID) missions can have long-term benefits. A sergeant that a SF team trains in patrolling today may be a

across Europe has been replaced with discussions of Operations Other Than War (OOTW) and Small Scale Contingencies.

As the years have gone by the Special Forces have adapted to the geopolitical nature of warfare.

Special Forces ODAs are heavily engaged throughout the world. They are a highly relevant force of choice when circumstances require the use of small specialized teams. Capable of easy transition from peacetime to conflict, the SF teams are known as the "Quiet Professionals." These low-key forces are earning trust, building relationships, and establishing credibility around the world.

future colonel. That captain with whom they share a Meal Ready to Eat may someday be the leader of the country. By teaching these countries how to defend themselves, it may mean the United States does not have deploy multiple divisions of troops to an area. Establishing a warrior bond with these host nation soldiers may very likely create a strong ally for the United States in the future.

In addition to mastering the established conventional skills and military occupational specialties, SF soldiers are taught many special skills to develop the unique proficiencies that give them a wide variety of capabilities. They stand ready to execute their missions in any environment by any means of infiltration, air, land, or sea. This sergeant from the 7th Special Forces Groups (Airborne) in HALO equipment is ready to jump in to perform an FID, UW, SR, DA, or any other mission he is tasked.

The M2 Selectable Lightweight Attack Munition, or SLAM. Weighing a mere 2.2 pounds and small enough to fit in a BDU pocket, it is a low-volume, multipurpose munition. The M2 is self-contained, can be easily emplaced, and is compatible with other munitions for anti-material, anti-vehicular, and anti-personnel uses. It has four detonation modes, passive IR, magnetic influence, time delay, and command detonation.

Part of the Special Operation Forces Demolition Kit. This kit provides the SF soldier the capability to custom build, attach, and waterproof demolitions charges for specific target and operational scenarios. Seen here is the Explosive Form Penetration device or EFP. The device is packed with C4, thus creating a shaped explosive charge. For stability and deployment, it is placed upon a tripod. The EFP has a picatinny rail on the top; this allows an aiming device, such as an Aimpoint, in this case, to be attached. Once the target has been sighted in, the optical sight is removed and the EFP is set for detonation. This explosive device will penetrate concrete walls or rolled hardened armor.

I am an American Special Forces soldier. A professional! I will do all that my nation requires of me.

I am a volunteer, knowing well the hazards of my profession.

I serve with the memory of those who have gone before me: Rogers' Rangers, Francis Marion, Mosby's Rangers, the First Special Service Forces and Ranger Battalions of World War II, the Airborne Ranger Companies of Korea. I pledge to uphold the honor and integrity of all I am—in all I do.

I am a professional soldier. I will teach and fight wherever my nation requires. I will strive always to excel in every art and artifice of war.

I know that I will be called upon to perform tasks in isolation, far from familiar faces and voices, with the help and guidance of my God.

I will keep my mind and body clean, alert, and strong, for this is my debt to those with whom I serve. I will not bring shame upon myself or the forces.

I will maintain myself, my arms, and my equipment in an immaculate state as befits a Special Forces soldier.

I will never surrender though I be the last. If I am taken, I pray that I may have the strength to spit upon my enemy.

My goal is to succeed in any mission—and live to succeed again.

I am a member of my nation's chosen soldiery. God grant that I may not be found wanting, that I will not fail this sacred trust.

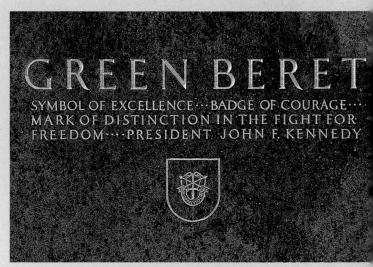

The Green Beret is more than a headgear issued to graduates of the Q-Course. Today, as when it was adopted, it stands for liberty, freedom, and professionalism. The SF soldier who dons a beret colored forest green is a diplomat, a soldier, and a warrior. Ask a collection of SF soldiers, and they will tell you, "the beret is hot in the summer, and cold in the winter; but don't even think of taking it away. It's like the flag."

The RQ-1A Predator is a medium-altitude, long-endurance Unmanned Aerial Vehicle or UAV. This aerial craft is considered a joint forces air component, and is deployed for reconnaissance, surveillance, and target acquisition in support of the Joint Force Commander. More than a mere aircraft, the Predator is a system, equipped with color camera in the nose, a day variable aperture television camera, a variable aperture infrared camera (for low light/night). It is also equipped with a synthetic aperture radar for looking through smoke, clouds, and haze. The Predator UAV system can provide real-time imaging that will assist in the often unique missions tasked to Special Forces ODAs. *Photograph provided by General Atomics Aeronautical Systems, Inc.*

Good intelligence can mean the difference between success or failure, life or death, on the battlefield. Information Dominance is a focus of new technology to keep the Special Forces at the leading edge. Referred to as "Ground Truth," officially it is called "IT-21" for Information Technology for the 21st Century. It is designed to enhance Command and Control, Communication, Computers and Intelligence (C4I), and to ensure connectivity with joint, combined, and coalition forces, while maintaining situational awareness.

Today's SF team will deploy with the latest state-of-the-art equipment, yet it is constantly looking at ways to improve its edge in combat. For this purpose, U.S. Army Special Operations Command (USASOC) has Lieutenant Colonel Daniel Moore, the G-7, Force Integration. The job of the G-7 is strategic planning, force structure, and equipment for the next decade to ensure the ODAs are appropriately equipped to meet future contingencies. From thermal underwater to body armor, from remote reconnaissance camera systems to complex combat simulations, if it will enhance the ODA, you'll find a file covering it on the G-7s PC.

New explosive devices are finding their way into the rucksacks of current SF ODAs—items like the M2 SLAM, or Selectable Lightweight Attack Munitions. The SLAM weighs a mere 2.2 pounds and is small enough to fit in the pocket of a battle dress uniform (BDU). The explosively formed penetrating warhead can pierce targets of 40mm rolled homogeneous armor out to 25 feet. It has four operating modes: Bottom attack (magnetic influence fuse)—as a vehicle passes over the M2, it will sense the magnetic signature and will detonate upward; Side attack (passive IR)—detonation occurs when sensing a passing vehicle's infrared signature; Time demolition of a target in four settings—15, 30, 45, and 60 minutes; and finally, Operator-initiated command detonation, using the standard Army blasting caps with the new time delay firing device (TDFD).

Another useful explosive device is the M150 Penetration Augmented Munition (PAM). The PAM is a lightweight man portable demolition device developed for special operations forces. It is compact at 33 inches, weighs 35 pounds, and can be emplaced by a single SF soldier. The primary use of the munition is against reinforced concrete bridge supports, piers, walls, and abutments. The munition can easily be carried in the rucksack or affixed to the soldier's Load Bearing Equipment without restricting his ability to walk, climb, rappel, or fast rope. It can be ignited by any standard military detonation device.

The PAM is hung against the target. The warhead consists of a forward charge, which cuts any rebar; a hole-drilling charge, which forms a hole in the target; and a follow-through charge, which is propelled to the bottom of the hole where it detonates. The explosion fractures the structure and results in a loss of at least 75 percent of the load-bearing capacity. The PAM's efficiency at destabilizing a structure allows two SF soldiers with two PAM units (70 pounds) to set up the devices and be ready to exfil in two minutes.

In the realm of information dominance, the G-7 shop is looking at the use of Unmanned Aerial Vehicles, or UAVs, to provide up-to-the-minute

Currently under consideration for possible addition to the SOPMOD kit is the Lightweight Shotgun System or LSS. Similar to the M-203, 40mm Grenade launcher, the LSS would be mounted under the barrel of the M4A1 Carbine. The LSS is a 12-gauge weapon that would most likely be carried by the point man, giving him an extra punch. It would also prove useful in the Special Forces Advanced Urban Combat role and Close Quarters Battle operations. *USASOC*

With the demise of the Soviet Union, the world is seeing numerous wannabe dictators and terrorist threats to U.S. and allied interests alike. The U.S. Army Special Forces are prepared for such contingency operations. By training its soldiers in the Special Forces Advance Reconnaissance, Target Analysis, and Exploitation Techniques Course, USASOC is mission capable of handling any threat. Pictured here is a terrorist's worst nightmare, a SFARTAETC trained stack ready to perform a dynamic entry.

aerial reconnaissance of the battlefield. A prime example of such a craft is the RQ-1A Predator UAV, manufactured by General Atomics Aeronautical Systems Inc. The Predator is a medium-altitude, long-endurance UAV. It is a Joint Forces Air Component Commander–owned theater asset for reconnaissance, surveillance, and target acquisition in support of the Joint Force command. The Predator UAV is equipped with a color nose camera, a day variable aperture TV camera, a variable aperture infrared camera for low light/night, and a synthetic aperture radar, for looking through smoke, clouds, or haze. The camera produces full-motion video and SAR still-frame radar images. The three sensors are carried on the same air frame but cannot be operated simultaneously. With a speed of 80 miles per hour and a range of 400 nautical miles, the Predator can loiter up to 25,000 feet for a period of 24 hours. With a gross weight of 2,250 pounds, this is definitely a support aircraft. However, USASOC is looking at the feasibility of small UAVs that could be carried into enemy territory in a rucksack. The small hand-held versions of the UAV could provide the team with immediate imaging of their AO.

Along with the UAV and numerous satellites with Multi-speed Transient Imaging (MTI), Multi-Hyper Spectral Imaging (HSI), and Synthetic Aperture Radar (SAR), NASA's shuttle missions have been used to map the world to within a meter. When you combine all of this input and run it through a simulator, you have an extremely accurate view of your target area. Throw in some blueprints and 3-D modeling software and you now have a full mission profile from insertion to exfil, all inside the computer. Teams can use such a simulation to actually plan their missions: What is the best route in? There, from the Northwest. Where is the best vantage point for the sniper? There, just beyond that outcropping of rocks. The team can even enter the building and recon, all from the safety of the simulator in the Isolation Facility. It is called "Virtual Recon." The unclassified look was amazing—one can only imagine what the classified version looks like.

Communications devices will also get a revamping as the technology improves. Eventually, we'll see the iridium phone and radio technology becoming so prevalent that instead of an ODA carrying a large PSC-5 and MBIIT radios, each SF soldier will have his own personal communication device small enough to fit into the pocket of the rucksack, or in an M16 magazine pouch. The device will have all the current features, including SATCOM communications with the Mission Support Site, CinC, group, or even National Command Authority, if necessary, all on a secure uplink.

One last item from the G-7 shop is fused imaging. This technology will combine thermal imaging with image intensifiers, day/night vision, integrated HUD (Heads Up Display) with a laser target reticle of the weapon, and a Global Positioning System microchip, all in one set of glasses. All of this technology is here today; it is just a matter of time before it is incorporated into a working unit.

Without a doubt USSOCOM and USASOC provide the best weapons and equipment for the men of the Special Forces Groups. Their efforts are paramount in providing the SF soldier with what is necessary not only for mission success, but also personnel survival. However, it is still the man on the ground that makes the difference— the sergeant who hoists a 150-pound rucksack on his back; the SFC who serves as the only U.S. military presence in a foreign country; the ODA that HALOs out of an MC-130 and lives in the bush for weeks, months, or longer. You only have to spend a short amount of time with the men who wear that woolen headgear and have that tab on their shoulder to understand that the Green Berets are warriors par excellence. Whether equipped with the SOPMOD M4A1, a SLAM and a UAV overhead, or a K-Bar, a block of C4, and a map, the SF soldier will execute his mission.

A command brief from the 7th SFG(A) lists the following SOF Truths: Humans are more important than hardware. Quality is better than quantity. Special Operations Forces cannot be mass produced. And, competent Special Operations Forces cannot be created after emergencies occur. With the experience gained over the years through sweat and blood, continuing in the heritage of those who have gone before, the Special Forces soldiers are trained, prepared, and equipped to operate in any environment, anywhere on the globe, anytime they are needed.

The Special Forces are a lethal, intelligent, decisive, and high-risk force for combat. Whenever needed, they will be ready to answer the call. The green beret remains "the symbol of excellence, a badge of courage" for the "Quiet Professionals" of the U.S. Army Special Forces.

Steeped in the heritage of the last five decades . . . armed with the lessons of those who gave the ultimate sacrifice . . . trained to master the art and science of unconventional warfare . . . ever vigilant to their creed and the motto, "De Opresso Liber," To Free The Oppressed: The men of the U.S. Army Special Forces remain the tip of the spear.

Glossary of Terms

AT: Antiterrorism. Defensive measures used to reduce the vulnerability of individuals and property to terrorism.

C4I: Command, Control, Communications, Computers, and Intelligence.

CinC: Commander in Chief.

Civil Affairs: The activities of a commander that establish, maintain, influence, or exploit relations between military forces and civil authorities, both governmental and nongovernmental, and the civilian population in a friendly, neutral, or hostile area of operations in order to facilitate military operations and consolidate operational objectives. Civil Affairs may include performance by military forces of activities and functions normally the responsibility of the local government. These activities may occur prior to, during, or subsequent to military action. They may also occur, if directed, in the absence of other military operations.

Clandestine Operation: Activities sponsored or conducted by governmental departments or agencies in such a way as to ensure secrecy or concealment. (It differs from covert operations in that emphasis is placed on concealment of the operation rather than on concealment of identity of sponsor.) In Special Operations, an activity may be both covert and clandestine and may focus equally on operational considerations and intelligence-related activities.

Close Air Support (CAS): Air action against hostile targets that are in close proximity to friendly forces. Each action requires detailed integration with the fire and movement of those forces.

Collateral special operations activities: Collateral activities in which Special Operations forces, by virtue of their inherent capabilities, may be selectively tasked to participate. The activities may include security assistance, humanitarian assistance, antiterrorism and other security activities, counter-drug operations, personnel recovery, and special activities.

Counterproliferation: Activities taken to counter the spread of dangerous military capabilities, allied technologies and/or know-how, especially weapons of mass destruction and ballistic missile delivery systems.

Counterterrorism: Offensive measures taken to prevent, deter, and respond to terrorism.

Covert Operations: Operations that are planned and executed so as to conceal the identity of, or permit plausible denial by, the sponsor.

Crisis: An incident or situation involving a threat to the United States, its territories, citizens, military forces and possessions or vital interests that develops rapidly and creates a condition of such diplomatic, economic, political, or military importance that commitment of U.S. military forces and resources is contemplated to achieve national objectives.

Direct action mission: In special operations, a specific act involving operations of an overt, covert, clandestine, or low-visibility nature conducted primarily by a sponsoring power's special operations forces in hostile or denied areas.

Ducks - Types of Zodiac deployments.
    Double: Twin Zodiacs
    Hard: Zodiac with hard metal bottom
    Soft: Zodiac raft

Exfiltration (Exfil): The removal of personnel or units from areas under enemy control.

First Line Belt: Specially designed webbing with shock cord inside, used when traveling on aircraft. One end has a standard carabiner, and the other end a quick-release carabiner.

Foreign Internal Defense (FID): Participation by civilian and military agencies of a government in any action programs taken by another government to free and protect its society from subversion, lawlessness, and insurgency.

Guerrilla Warfare: Military and paramilitary operations conducted in enemy-held or hostile territory by irregular, predominantly indigenous forces.

Host Nation: A nation that receives the forces and/or supplies of allied nations and/or NATO organizations to be located on, operate in, or transit through its territory.

Humanitarian assistance: Assistance provided by Department of Defense forces, as directed by appropriate authority, in the aftermath of natural or manmade disasters to help reduce conditions that present a serious threat to life and property. Assistance provided by U.S. forces is limited in scope and duration and is designed to supplement efforts of civilian authorities that have primary responsibility for providing such assistance.

Infiltration (Infil): The movement through or into an area or territory occupied by either friendly or enemy troops or organizations. The movement is made either by small groups or by individuals at extended or irregular intervals. When used in connection with the enemy, it implies that contact is avoided.

Insurgency: An organized movement aimed at the overthrow of a constituted government through the use of subversion and armed conflict.

Internal defense: The full range of measures taken by a government to free and protect its society from subversion, lawlessness, and insurgency.

Inter-operability: The ability of systems, units, or forces to provide services to and to accept services from other systems, units, or forces and use the services so exchanged to enable them to operate effectively together.

Low-intensity conflict: Political-military confrontation between contending states or groups below conventional war and above routine, peaceful competition among states. It frequently involves protracted struggles of competing principles and ideologies. Low-intensity conflict ranges from subversion to the use of armed force. It is waged by a combination of means employing political, economic, informational, and military instruments. Low-intensity conflicts are often localized, generally in the Third World, but contain regional and global security implications.

Maquis: Active guerrilla groups, World War II.

Military Civic Action: The use of indigenous military forces on projects useful to the local population at all levels in such fields as education, training, public works, agriculture, transportation, communications, health, sanitation and others contributing to economic and social development.

Mission: A statement of an entity's reason for being and what it wishes to accomplish as an organization.

Nation Assistance: Civil and/or military assistance rendered to a nation's territory during peacetime, crises, or emergencies, or war, based on agreements mutually concluded between nations. Nation Assistance programs include, but are not limited to, security assistance, FID, other DOD Title 10 programs, and activities performed on a reimbursable basis by federal agencies or international organizations.

NCA: National Command Authority. The President and the Secretary of Defense together, or their duly deputized alternates or successors. The term signifies constitutional authority to direct the Armed Forces in their execution of military action.

Objectives: Specific actions to be achieved in a specified time period. Accomplishment will indicate progress toward achieving the goals.

Operator: See "Shooter."

Psychological operations: Planned operations to convey selected information and indicators to foreign audiences to influence their emotions, motives, and objective reasoning, and ultimately the behavior of foreign government, organizations, groups, and individuals. The purpose of psychological operations is to induce or reinforce foreign attitudes and behavior favorable to the originator's objectives.

Ranger Assist Cord: 550 parachute line, used to attach anything and everything to an operator.

Shooter: Special Operations Forces trooper, e.g., U.S. Army Special Forces, U.S. Navy SEAL, U.S. Army Ranger, SAS (British or Australian), etc.

Special Reconnaissance: Reconnaissance and surveillance actions conducted by special operations forces to obtain or verify, by visual observation or other collection methods, information concerning the capabilities, intentions, and activities of an actual or potential enemy or to secure data concerning the meteorological, hydrographic, or geographic characteristics of a particular area. It includes target acquisition, area assessment, and post-strike reconnaissance.

Strategy: Methods, approaches, or specific moves taken to implement and attain an objective.

Unconventional Warfare (UW): A broad spectrum of military and paramilitary operations conducted in enemy-held, enemy-controlled, or politically sensitive territory. Unconventional warfare includes, but is not limited to, the interrelated fields of guerrilla warfare, evasion and escape, subversion, sabotage, and other operations of a low visibility, covert, or clandestine nature. These interrelated aspects of UW may be prosecuted singularly or collectively by predominantly indigenous personnel, usually supported and directed in varying degrees by (an) external source(s) during all conditions of war or peace.

Abbreviations

ARSOC	Army Special Operations Command		LZ	Landing Zone
AT-4	Anti-Tank Weapon		MFP	Major Force Program
CAS	Close Air Support		MGF	Mobile Guerrilla Force
CIA	Central Intelligence Agency		MPU	Message Pickup
COIN	Counterinsurgency		MRE	Meal Ready to Eat
COMINT	Communications Intelligence		MTT	Mobile Training Team
CSAR	Combat Search And Rescue		NOD	Night Optical Device
CT	Counterterrorism		NVG	Night Vision Goggles
CQB	Close Quarters Battle		OPCON/M	Operational Control/Command
DA	Direct Action		OPSEC	Operational Security
DAM/T	Direct Action Mission/Team		PSYWAR	Psychological Warfare
DIA	Defense Intelligence Agency		SEAL	Sea Air Land (U.S. Navy Special
DOD	Department of Defense			Operations Forces)
DZ	Drop Zone		SAR	Search and Rescue
E&E	Evasion and Escape		SAS	Special Air Service
ELINT	Electronic Intelligence		SBS	Special Boat Squadron
FID	Foreign Internal Defense		SF	Special Forces (U.S. Army)
FOB	Forward Operation Base		SFAUC	Special Forces Advanced Urban Combat
FOI	Forward Operating Location		SFARTAETC	Special Forces Advanced Reconnaissance,
FRIES	Fast Rope Insertion/Extraction System			Target Analysis & Exploitation Techniques
GPS	Global Positioning System			Course
HAHO	High Altitude High Opening		SFOB	Special Forces Operating Base
HALO	High Altitude Low Opening		SOCOM	Special Operations Command
HE	High Explosive		SOF	Special Operations Forces
HUD	Heads Up Display		SOFLAM	Special Operations Forces Laser
HUMINT	Human Intelligence			Acquisition Marker
INTREP	Intelligence Report		SR	Special Reconnaissance
JCS	Joint Chiefs of Staff		SWS	Sniper Weapon System
JSOC	Joint Special Operations Command		USASOC	U.S. Army Special Operations Command
JSOF	Joint Special Operations Forces		USASFC	U.S. Army Special Forces Command
JSOTF	Joint Special Operations Task Force		UW	Unconventional Warfare
JUWTF	Joint Unconventional Warfare Task Force		WM	Weapons of Mass Destruction
LBE	Load Bearing Equipment			

Index

U.S. Air Force Special Ops
ISBN: 0-7603-0733-4

America's Special Forces
ISBN: 0-7603–0366-5

Inside the U.S. Navy SEAL
ISBN: 0-7603-0178-6

**Buddies: Men, Dogs,
and World War II**
ISBN: 0-7603-1020-3

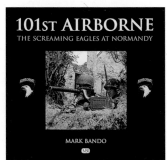

**101st Airborne:
The Screaming Eagles at Normandy**
ISBN: 0-7603-0855-1

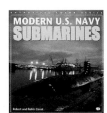

**Modern U.S. Navy
Submarines**
ISBN: 0-7603-0276-6

Lockheed Secret Projects
ISBN: 0-7603-0914-0

**Battlestations! American
Warships of World War II**
ISBN: 0-7603-0954-X

Pedal Cars
ISBN: 0-8793-8955-9